Collins

Enriching English 6

READER

Radhika Tadepalli
Somali Mitra

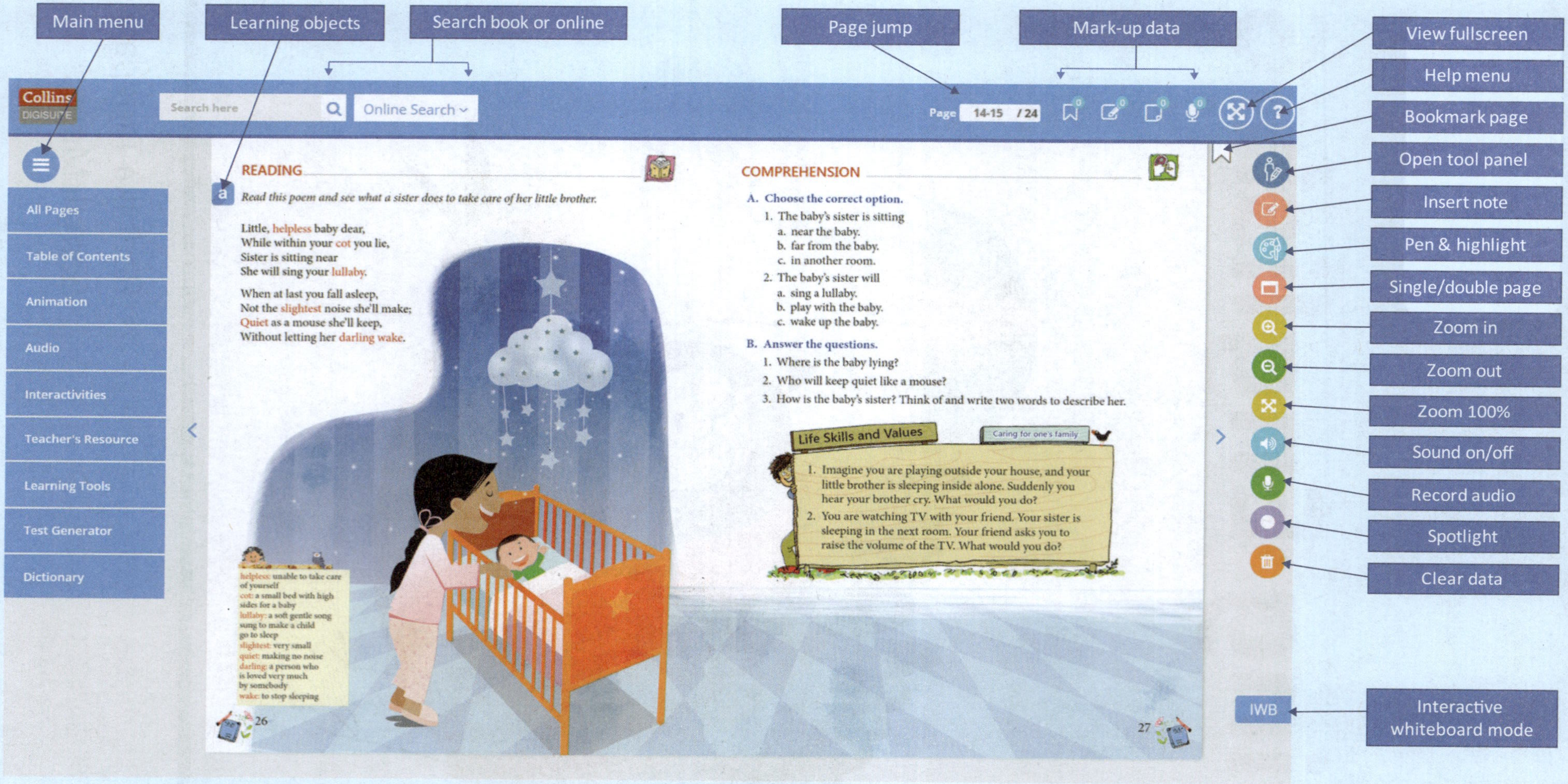

Student + Teacher			Teacher-only	
a animations	**ia** activities	**g** games	**lp** lesson plans	**tn** teacher's notes
ilt instructor-led tutorials	**w** worksheets	**v** videos	**w** worksheets	**ak** answer keys
	audio			

Preface

Literature as an area of study offers a unifying perspective of the world around us. It acts as a prism through which we can view every sphere of human civilization, including history and the sciences.

Enriching English is a language-through-literature course which is designed to introduce students to this larger world through a variety of literary works authored by Indian and global writers. In doing so, it also aims to build the foundations of English language learning by introducing students to the formal structures that enable language acquisition.

The series comprises graded Readers and Language Companions, with support material in the form of Teacher's Resource Books and enhanced digital learning resources.

Readers

The Readers offer a wide variety of engaging literary texts organized thematically. Each unit in the Reader is built around a distinct theme, ranging from family and friendship, to wildlife and outer space. It usually includes a prose and a poetry chapter.

The units begin with **Take Off**, a warm-up section drawn from the theme and related to the reading passages in the units. This section is used for pre-teaching vocabulary to be encountered in the reading passage while drawing on the learner's knowledge of his immediate environment and the larger world. It also includes speaking and writing tasks.

The **reading passages** comprise an eclectic selection of texts, ranging from the classic to the contemporary and include short stories, excerpts from well-known novels, non-fiction passages, poems and plays. They cover a variety of literary genres such as folktale, fable, short story, nonsense poetry as well as extracts from popular novels like *Harry Potter and the Half-Blood Prince*. Each book also includes a graphic story, often a retelling of a well-known folktale, mythological tale or an episode from a novel.

The passages are also interspersed with related trivia in **Food for thought**, and contextual explanations for literary devices and figures of speech in **Literary terms**. Contextually drawn **Common idioms and proverbs**, meant to enhance students' vocabulary, are also covered. A short **biography** introduces students to the author of the passage.

Comprehension includes both factual and inferential questions. Short exercises and 'reference to context' questions check factual understanding of the text. **Life skills and Values** includes interpretative and analytical questions which build students' higher order thinking skills while honing their understanding of human values and developing the right attitudes in them.

Vocabulary comprises exercises based on contextual usage and extended word building tasks. It also tests students' understanding of literary devices and figures of speech encountered in the passage.

Grammar includes simple explanations of language structures followed by practice tasks showing graded progression. Tree maps and tables illustrate concepts for easy comprehension.

Study Skills covers the sub-skills of language acquisition and includes phonics and spelling drills as well as dictionary referencing tasks. Special attention is also given to familiarizing students with the use of online dictionaries.

Listening develops aural comprehension skills through various kinds of factual questions.

Speaking covers conversation and role play activities to enable students to respond appropriately in a variety of social situations. It also includes public speaking activities and group discussions.

Writing includes guided and free writing exercises that develop functional and creative writing skills.
The **Activity** in the poetry chapters includes exercises which combine hands-on tasks with creative writing skills. Every task includes plenty of scaffolding in the form of suggested vocabulary and reference samples.

Now I can … is a self-assessment checklist for the learner to examine whether they have met the learning objectives for the lesson.

Read at Leisure includes suggestions for further reading related to the author or theme of the reading passage.

Projects, of which there are three, revisit the themes covered in each book. They encourage students to correlate the themes with the world around them through a mix of simple research-based tasks and creative thinking.

A **glossary of literary terms and genres** at the end of the book acts as a ready reference.

Language Companions

The Language Companions complement the Readers. They have been designed to provide practice to the students in the language skills required to excel in the formal examination. They are closely linked to the units in the Reader and cover reading comprehension passages and guided writing tasks besides grammar and vocabulary. The Companions can also act as a self-study tool, providing materials for further practice.

Teacher's Resource Books

The Teacher's Resource Books are designed to facilitate teachers so that they can make the best use of the material given in the books to achieve the objectives set out in the curriculum. They include activity-based lesson plans, additional worksheets on each area of language learning, answer keys to the Readers as well as the listening texts for the aural tasks in the Readers.

Digital Resources

The Collins DigiSuite DVD comprises:

- the Reader given as a **multimedia e-book**, which also includes the complete audio of the reading passages as well as interactive exercises
- **Language Games**, **Picture Dictionary** and a level-appropriate **Collins dictionary** for further practice
- **Test Generator** for quick creation of assignments and test papers
- the **Teacher's Resource Book** in digital format

We hope that this series fosters a love for literature and makes students aware of the many nuances that language lends itself to, while equipping them with the formal language acquisition skills to express themselves correctly in the English language.

Authors

Acknowledgements

The publishers wish to thank and acknowledge the following for granting us permission to use copyright material:

Sudha Murty for *How I Taught My Grandmother to Read*. Reprinted with the permission of the author; Ruskin Bond for *Children of India*. Reprinted with the permission of the author; *The Power of Music* by Sukumar Ray. Reproduced with permission of Oxford University Press India © Oxford University Press 1987; *An Unexpected Guest* from *My Family and Other Animals* by Gerald Durrell. Reproduced with permission of Curtis Brown Group Ltd, London on behalf of Lee Durrell as the Beneficiary of The Estate of Gerald Durrell. Copyright © Gerald Durrell 1956; *Hunting Snake*, taken from *Collected Poems* by Judith Wright, reprinted with permission of HarperCollins Publishers Australia; *The People Upstairs*, copyright © 1949 by Ogden Nash, renewed. Reprinted by permission of Curtis Brown, Ltd.; *The Theft of the Ruby*, reprinted by permission of HarperCollins Publishers Ltd © 1923 Agatha Christie; Aaron Shepard for *The Christmas Truce*. Reprinted with the permission of the author.

The publishers have applied for permission for the following:
A Hero by R. K. Narayan; *A Day's Wait* by Ernest Hemingway; *The Doctor* by Sir Alan Patrick Herbert; *I Wave Good-bye When Butter Flies* by Jack Prelutsky.
Acknowledgements for these texts will be made in the future editions of the book.

Every effort has been made to trace copyright holders and to obtain their permission for the use of copyright material. However, in some instances, we have been unable to trace the owners of the copyright pieces published here. The authors and publishers will gladly receive any information enabling them to rectify any error or omission in subsequent editions.

Cover: MashaStarus/iStockphoto.

Inside: Page 20: pe-art **21:** graphic-bee **23:** Mykhailo Ridkous **27:** quisp65 **28:** eliflamra, ikryannikovgmailcom **33:** colematt **34:** viyadaistock **35:** Ofeliya-o-nimf **44:** pukrufus **45:** Vect0r0vich **46:** Irina_Stankevich, Dar_ria **48:** Hulton Archive/Stringer, Lisa Maree Williams/Stringer, PictureLake, mattjeacock, Bettmann/Contributor **54:** Le_Mon **55:** TopVectors **56:** engabito **57:** Monica Smile, danbailey **63:** cosmaa **66:** kbeis, catsinside, IconicBestiary, eliflamra, Leonhartrizal, pijama61 **72:** colematt **74:** InfiniteGraphic **80:** Goddard_Photography, siridhata, AYImages, 4FR, sandf320, Searsie, erwinf, LagunaticPhoto **88:** Tat'yana Mazitova, m-e-l **89:** Btownchris, alashi **93:** jetFoto, JoeLena **96:** aomist, Tomacco **103:** askmenow **107:** ndesign, Enis Aksoy, sabelskaya, Astragal **109:** PANKAJ JAGYA, **110:** kbeis, Bob_Eastman **111:** aqabiz, eliflamra **118:** Bannosuke, **120:** kristijánh, ksenya_savva **121:** alexokokok **122:** aqabiz **125:** Salvadorova **126:** TatianaNikulina **127:** wynnter **131:** dja65 **136:** kbeis, ariadnaS **137:** Stock Ninja Studio **142:** SmallArtFish **143:** Branchegevara **144:** Praveena Bhagwat **145:** Mail Today/Contributor **146:** CARL COURT/Stringer **148:** KALLE PARKKINEN/Contributor **149:** Garret48 **151:** JaaakWorks, sabelskaya **152:** lvcandy, **156:** subarashii21, artisticco **157:** divyesh kachhdiya **158:** PenWin, Olga_Z, Stu Forster/Staff

Poster: skeeg, Ajwad Creative, Hulton Archive/Stringer, ilbusca, Ronald Dumont/Stringer, mammoth, MaryValery

Key Features

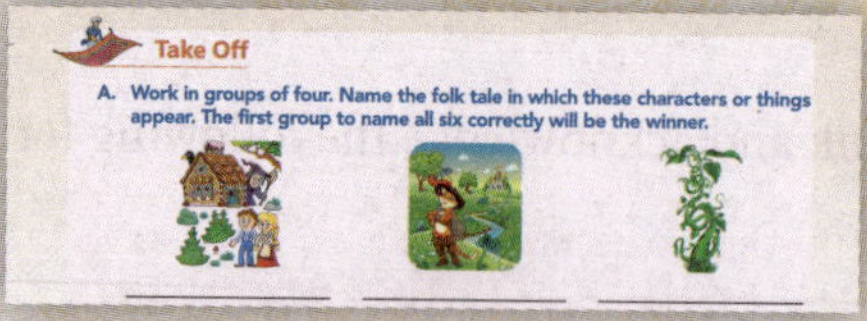

Take Off has theme-based warm-up activities

Reading comprises a rich variety of texts by global and Indian writers

Food for thought, Literary terms, Common idioms and proverbs have additional trivia, explanations of figures of speech, idiomatic structures and proverbs

Glossary includes contextual meanings of difficult words

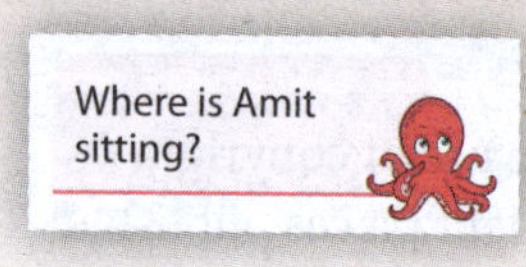

While-reading **in-text questions** check factual understanding

About the author/poet includes a brief biography of the author/poet

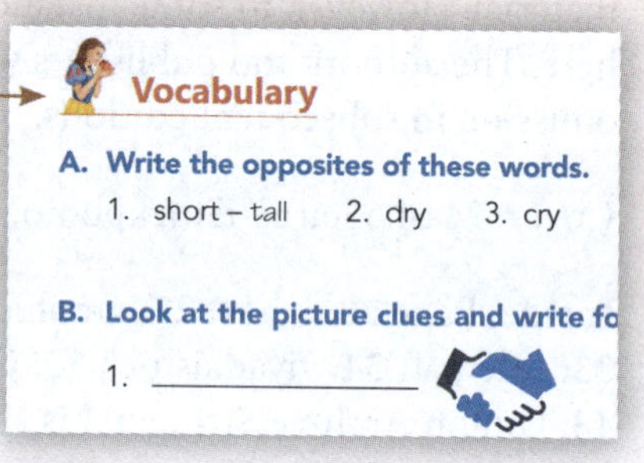

Comprehension checks factual understanding through 'wh-' and 'reference-to-the-context' questions

Vocabulary includes exercises on contextual usage, modes of vocabulary acquisition and figures of speech

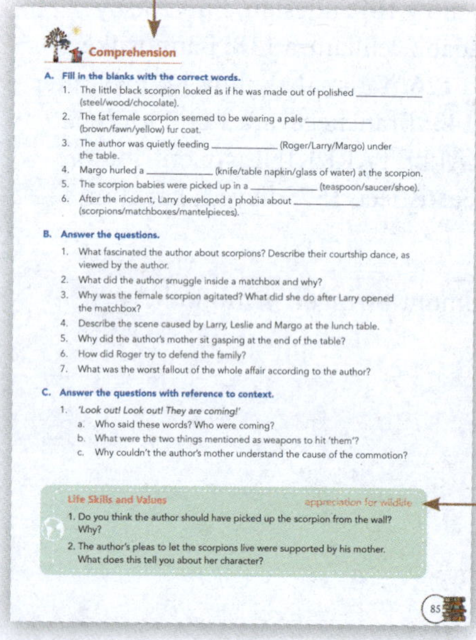

The **Life skills and Values** section has inferential questions on moral values and interpersonal skills

Grammar includes graded practice tasks accompanied by simple explanations

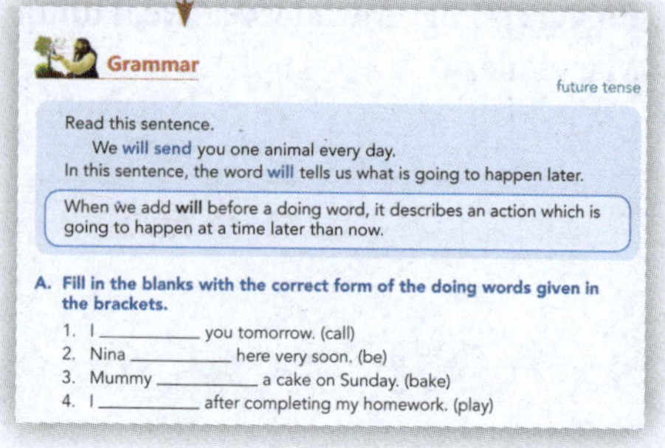

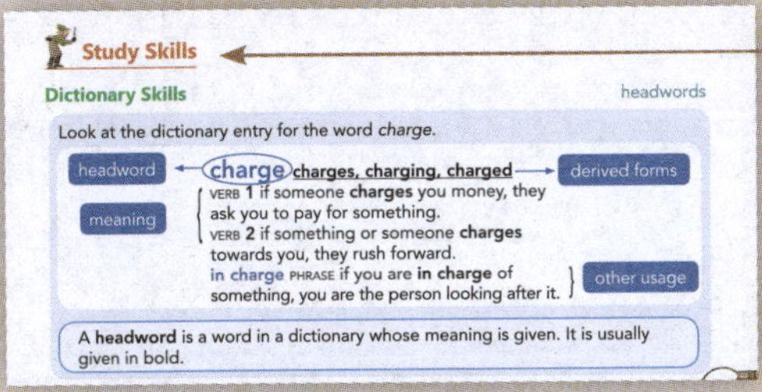
Study Skills

Dictionary Skills — headwords

Look at the dictionary entry for the word *charge*.

headword — charge — charges, charging, charged — derived forms

meaning — VERB 1 if someone **charges** you money, they ask you to pay for something. VERB 2 if something or someone **charges** towards you, they rush forward.

in charge PHRASE if you are **in charge** of something, you are the person looking after it. — other usage

A **headword** is a word in a dictionary whose meaning is given. It is usually given in bold.

Study Skills includes graded phonics, spelling and dictionary activities

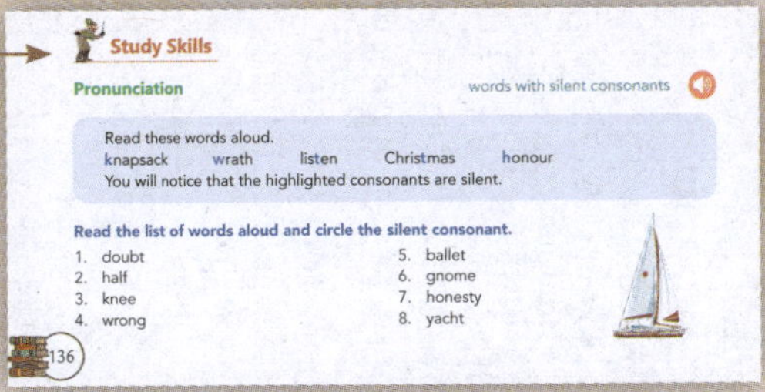
Study Skills

Pronunciation — words with silent consonants

Read these words aloud.
knapsack wrath listen Christmas honour
You will notice that the highlighted consonants are silent.

Read the list of words aloud and circle the silent consonant.

1. doubt
2. half
3. knee
4. wrong
5. ballet
6. gnome
7. honesty
8. yacht

136

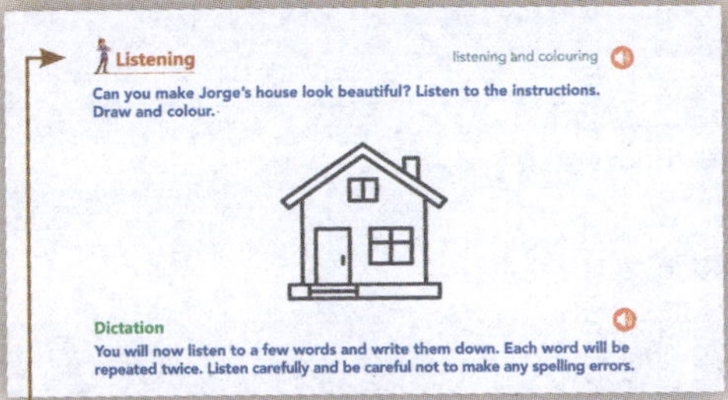
Listening — listening and colouring

Can you make Jorge's house look beautiful? Listen to the instructions. Draw and colour.

Dictation

You will now listen to a few words and write them down. Each word will be repeated twice. Listen carefully and be careful not to make any spelling errors.

Writing includes graded and free writing tasks. Poetry chapters include **Activity**, a hands-on creative task

Listening covers aural comprehension activities, as well as word and sentence-based **Dictation** tasks

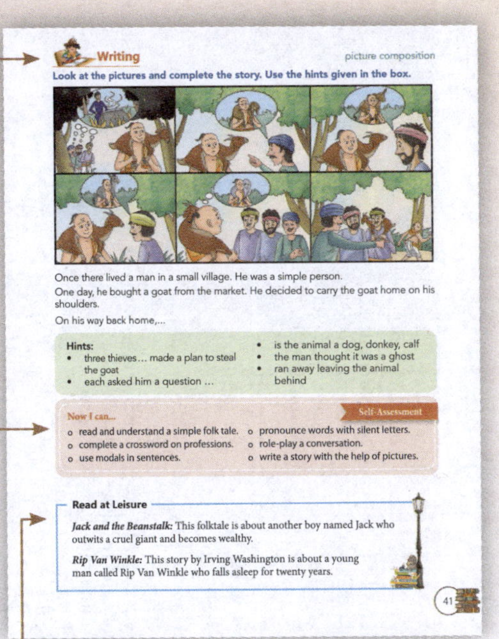
Writing — picture composition

Look at the pictures and complete the story. Use the hints given in the box.

Once there lived a man in a small village. He was a simple person.
One day, he bought a goat from the market. He decided to carry the goat home on his shoulders.
On his way back home,...

Hints:
- three thieves ... made a plan to steal the goat
- each asked him a question ...
- is the animal a dog, donkey, calf
- the man thought it was a ghost
- ran away leaving the animal behind

Now I can... — Self-Assessment
- read and understand a simple folk tale.
- complete a crossword on professions.
- use modals in sentences.
- pronounce words with silent letters.
- role-play a conversation.
- write a story with the help of pictures.

Read at Leisure

Jack and the Beanstalk: This folktale is about another boy named Jack who outwits a cruel giant and becomes wealthy.

Rip Van Winkle: This story by Irving Washington is about a young man called Rip Van Winkle who falls asleep for twenty years.

41

Speaking includes role plays, conversation practice and public speaking tasks through solo, pair and group work

Now I can ... is a self-assessment checklist at the end of every chapter

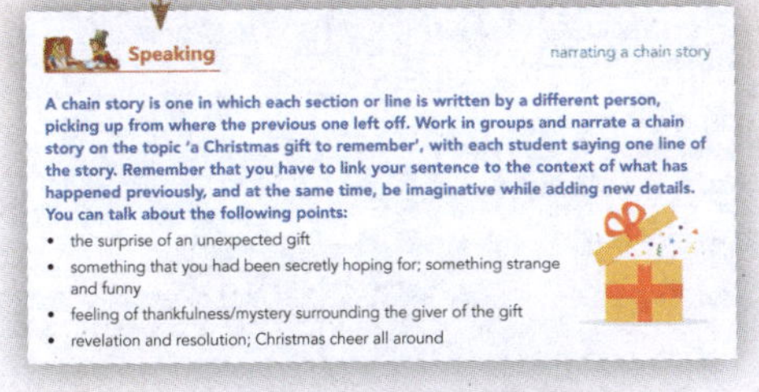
Speaking — narrating a chain story

A chain story is one in which each section or line is written by a different person, picking up from where the previous one left off. Work in groups and narrate a chain story on the topic 'a Christmas gift to remember', with each student saying one line of the story. Remember that you have to link your sentence to the context of what has happened previously, and at the same time, be imaginative while adding new details. You can talk about the following points:
- the surprise of an unexpected gift
- something that you had been secretly hoping for; something strange and funny
- feeling of thankfulness/mystery surrounding the giver of the gift
- revelation and resolution; Christmas cheer all around

Read at Leisure has suggestions for further reading

Cross-curricular **Projects** cover literature-based activities related to the themes in the book

Project 1

You have read about friendship in *A Cycle Race* and in *Raha's Birthday*. Friends are important. They share our joys and sorrows and help us become better.

Do you know that there is a special day to celebrate our friends?
It is called *Friendship Day*. It is celebrated on the first Sunday of August every year.

A. Write down the name of any two friends with whom you want to celebrate Friendship Day.

B. Make a friendship band using paper, string, and beads. Paste it here. You can take the help of your parents.

37

Posters explore new categories of literature in every class

Detailed Contents

Unit	Chapter	Reading Comprehension	Vocabulary	Grammar	Study Skills	Listening	Speaking	Writing	Activity
Imagination and Make-Believe	1. The Incident of the Tooth	• Flow chart • Questions • Reference to context • Inferential and extrapolative questions	• Idioms • Colloquialisms	• Nouns: countable, uncountable, singular and plural • Abstract nouns	• Pronunciation: long and short *i*	• Listening to a passage and gap filling • Dictation	• Think-pair-share	• Writing an informal letter	
	2. Silver	• MCQ • Reference to context • Inferential and extrapolative questions	• Crossword • Suffixes						• Speak-a-minute
Quest for Knowledge	3. How I Taught My Grandmother to Read	• True or false • Questions • Reference to context • Inferential and extrapolative questions	• Words related to books and reading • Forming antonyms with prefixes *dis-*, *un-*, *il-*	• Types of adjectives • Phrases and clauses	• Dictionary skills: synonyms	• Listening to a passage and gap filling	• Group discussion	• Writing a message	
	4. Children of India	• Tick the correct answer • Reference to context • Inferential and extrapolative questions	• Commonly confused words • Phrasal verbs	• Subject and predicate • Tenses: simple and continuous	• Spelling: names of professions using *-ian*, *-ist*, *-er*	• Listening to a passage and stating true or false	• Participating in a debate	• Descriptive and narrative essays	
Humour	5. A Hero	• MCQ • Character study • Reference to context • Inferential and extrapolative questions	• Contextual usage • Verbs indicating expressions	• Types of pronouns • Punctuation • Apostrophe to show possession	• Spelling: *ie* and *ei* words	• Listening to a passage and answering questions • Dictation	• Interview	• Writing a story • Writing a dialogue	
	6. The Power of Music	• Completing sentences • Reference to context • Inferential and extrapolative questions	• Compound nouns • Homonyms						• Recitation • Completing a fact sheet
Project 1									
Health and Hygiene	7. A Day's Wait	• True or false • Reference to context • Inferential and extrapolative questions	• Words related to health	• Direct and indirect speech • Subject-verb agreement	• Pronunciation: stressed and unstressed syllables	• Listening to a dialogue and answering questions	• Conversation: making and responding to suggestions	• Picture composition	
	8. The Doctor	• MCQ • Reference to context • Inferential and extrapolative questions	• Rhyme scheme						• Making a poster
Encounters with the Wild	9. An Unexpected Guest	• Fill in the blanks • Questions • Reference to context • Inferential and extrapolative questions	• Animal idioms • Similes	• Transitive and intransitive verbs • Types of adverbs and their positions	• Dictionary skills: finding meanings of words	• Listening to a poem and gap filling	• Expressing opinion	• Alternate ending to the story	
	10. Hunting Snake	• MCQ • Reference to context • Inferential and extrapolative questions	• Imagery						• Making a presentation

Community and Neighbourhood	11. A Spark Neglected Burns the House	• Questions • Reference to context • Inferential and extrapolative questions	• Synonyms • Proverbs	• Correlative conjunctions • Types of phrases	• Spelling: words with *-ary, -ery* and *-ory*	• Listening to a news article and completing sentences	• Role play: expressing emotions	• Writing a letter expressing regret	
	12. The People Upstairs	• Flow chart • Reference to context • Inferential and extrapolative questions	• *-ing* adjectives • Rhyme scheme						• Describing situations using figurative language
Project 2									
Food and Celebrations	13. The Theft of the Ruby	• Sequencing • Reference to context • Inferential and extrapolative questions	• Words related to celebrations • Verbs with similar meaning	• Tenses: perfect and perfect continuous • Auxiliary verbs	• Dictionary skills: words of French origin	• Listening to a passage and stating true or false • Dictation	• Enacting the story as a play	• Writing a notice • Writing an invitation	
	14. I Wave Good-bye When Butter Flies	• Completing sentences • Reference to context • Inferential and extrapolative questions	• Homophones • Pun						• Creating an advertisement
Tales of War	15. The Christmas Truce	• Questions • Reference to context • Inferential and extrapolative questions	• Contextual usage • Idioms related to army	• Types of sentences • Conditional sentences using *if* and *unless*	• Pronunciation: words with silent consonants	• Listening to a passage and gap filling	• Narrating a chain story	• Diary entry	
	16. After Blenheim	• One-word answers • Reference to context • Inferential and extrapolative questions	• Rhyming couplets • Repetition						• Researching and making a presentation
Overcoming Odds	17. India's Shining Girls	• Questions • Reference to context • Inferential and extrapolative questions	• Collocations • One-word substitutes	• Active and passive voice • Question tags	• Spelling: words with *au* sound	• Listening to a passage and answering questions	• Giving a speech	• Newspaper report	
	18. A Psalm of Life	• Completing the sentences • Reference to context • Inferential and extrapolative questions	• Metaphor • Archaic words						• Writing a poem
Project 3									
Literary Genres and Terms									

Contents

I

Imagination and Make-Believe

Take Off

A. Match these literary characters, known to make up tall stories and tell elaborate lies, with their descriptions.

Characters	Descriptions
1. Voldemort	a. This naughty wooden puppet is a habitual liar. Every time he lies, his nose grows longer. Woodpeckers are summoned to peck his nose and return it to its normal size.
2. Alice	b. This bored young girl finds her way to a fantasy world of talking animals and other fantastical creatures. Ultimately, the unreal world is revealed to be a dream.
3. Pinocchio	c. He loves having sugar, but repeatedly denies having it when asked by his father.
4. Sheriff of Nottingham	d. Skilled in dark magic, this leader of dark wizards will stop at no lie or deception to get what he wants: the young wizard who caused him to lose all his powers.
5. Johnny	e. The main villain in the *Robin Hood* stories, he always looks for opportunities to take money from the poor. Despite his attempts to deceive Robin Hood's band of outlaws, he is always outsmarted by them.

B. Do you think about imaginary things? Do everyday things turn magical in your imagination? Read these verses and identify the elements which are imaginary (not real). Then discuss them in groups.

1. Three of us afloat in the meadow by the swing,
Three of us aboard in the basket on the lea.
Winds are in the air, they are blowing in the spring,
And waves are on the meadow like the waves there are at sea.

2. 'Come, little leaves,'
Said the wind one day,
'Come over the meadows
With me, and play;
Put on your dresses
Of red and gold;
Summer is gone,
And the days grow cold.'

1 The Incident of the Tooth

Mark Twain

Reading

Have you ever made up a story so that you could skip school and stay home? This story is based on an extract from the book, The Adventures of Tom Sawyer, *set in the fictional town of St Petersberg in nineteenth century America. Tom is an orphan who lives with his Aunt Polly, his half-brother, Sid and his cousin Mary. Read on to find out what happens when Tom comes up with imaginative tales to avoid school.*

Monday morning found Tom Sawyer miserable. Monday morning always found him so— because it began another week's slow suffering in school.

Tom lay thinking. Presently it occurred to him that he wished he were sick; then he could stay home from school.

colicky: associated with a stomach ache
reflected: thought
hold in reserve: keep something available for later use
exertions: strenuous efforts
succession: (here) series

joggle: move; shake

window sash: window frame

handsomely: (here) successfully

rubbage: (here) rubbish

mortified: affected by gangrene, a serious condition which causes tissues in the body to decay

restored: brought back to normal condition

turn: a short period of feeling quite unwell

ceased: stopped

Food for thought

A common home remedy for removing a loose tooth was to tie a string to it and push a glowing coal towards the person's face. Fear of the burning coal would make their head jerk away. Meanwhile, the string, whose other end was tied to a stationery object, would pull the tooth in the opposite direction, thus getting it out.

row: (here) racket, noise

outrageousness: shocking acts that cross the limits of decency or reason

Common idioms and proverbs

play truant: This idiom means to stay away from school without permission or a genuine reason.

The tooth hung dangling by the bedpost.

But difficult times also bring their rewards. When Tom went to school later that day, he was the envy of every boy because the gap in his upper row of teeth allowed him to spit in a new way. He gathered quite a following of lads interested in the **exhibition**.

exhibition: display

About the author

Mark Twain (1835–1910), whose real name was Samuel Langhorne Clemens, was an American author best known for his books, *The Adventures of Tom Sawyer* and *The Adventures of Huckleberry Finn*. Twain based his books on his own childhood memories and experiences. The characters, Tom Sawyer and Huckleberry Finn became synonymous with mischief and pranks.

Comprehension

A. Complete the flow chart to show the order of events in the story.

1. Tom woke up one Monday morning, reluctant to attend school. He decided that the only way to stay home was to pretend to be ill.
2.
3. He looked at his sore toe and remembered an illness which could even make one lose a finger.
4.
5. After a lot of Tom's groaning and moaning, Sid finally woke up. He was scared because he thought that Tom was dying.

6

7 Aunt Polly realised that Tom was trying to fool her when he said that his toe was 'mortified'. Then he blurted out about his loose tooth.

8

B. Answer the questions.

1. Why did Tom dislike attending school on Mondays?
2. Why did Tom decide to hold the tooth in reserve? What did he then think of?
3. Why did Tom get annoyed with Sid?
4. What did Aunt Polly ask Mary to fetch?
5. According to Aunt Polly, what did Tom do to break her heart?
6. 'But difficult times also bring their rewards.' What was Tom's reward?
7. Do you think Aunt Polly was a sensible woman? Give reasons for your answer.

C. Answer the questions with reference to context.

1. *She laughed a little, then cried a little, then did both together.*
   a. Who is 'she' here? Why did she laugh and cry at the same time?
   b. What had Tom said to make her react in this way?
   c. Immediately after this, what did she tell Tom to do?
   d. What made Tom feel foolish?

Life Skills and Values — being responsible, honesty

1. Do you think it is important to consider how our actions can affect others? Explain with examples from the story.
2. Can lies be dangerous? Give reasons for your answer.
3. Did you think the story was funny? Which sections made you laugh? Explain in your own words.

Vocabulary

idioms

You know that an **idiom** is a group of words whose meaning is different from the meanings of the individual words. It is usually a combination of a noun and a verb.

Examples: It **makes my flesh crawl** to hear you. (= to feel afraid or horrified by something)

Tom, what **a turn you did give me**. (*give a turn* = frighten or shock somebody)

A. Match the idioms with their meanings.

Idioms	Meanings
1. have one's hands full	a. change one's way of life to become a better, more responsible person
2. spill the beans	b. not share the same views as somebody about something
3. turn over a new leaf	c. the benefits of two completely different situations at the same time
4. a bird's-eye view	d. very expensive
5. cost an arm and a leg	e. a view of something from a high position looking down
6. the best of both worlds	f. to be too busy to do something else
7. not see eye to eye with somebody	g. reveal a secret

Now, make sentences of your own with any three idioms.

colloquialisms

Read this line.

It **don't** hurt any more.

This is a colloquialism. Instead of using the grammatically correct verb *doesn't*, Tom uses the verb *don't*.

Look at some more examples.

Oh, Tom, you **ain't** dying, are you?

Are you **gonna** do the work or not?

Colloquialism is the informal use of language, often while speaking. It may include words which are grammatically incorrect, but which are nonetheless understood by the listeners.

B. Identify the colloquialisms in these sentences. Rewrite the colloquial words in correct English.

1. I ain't going to school tomorrow.
   I am not going to school tomorrow.
2. One of them dresses belongs to me.
3. They are gonna win the fight.
4. Wanna go to the park and play football?
5. I'll make y'all proud one day.
6. Gimme some bread and butter.
7. He don't come to school nowadays.

Grammar

nouns: countable and uncountable, singular and plural

Read this sentence.
Mary, get me some silk **threads**, and a chunk of **fire** out of the kitchen.

Here, the noun *thread* is **countable**. You know that countable nouns can be **singular** or **plural**. The word *fire* is an **uncountable noun**.

A. Identify the underlined nouns as countable (C) or uncountable (UC). Then rewrite the sentences, changing the singular countable nouns to their plural forms. You may have to make some necessary changes.

1. You can take a printout of this grammar worksheet and give it to the student.
   C; You can take printouts of these grammar worksheets and give them to the students.
2. Please pass the sugar.
3. The bakery makes fresh bread every morning.
4. They have built a new park in our neighbourhood.
5. I like having cereals with cold milk.
6. The newspaper reaches the hotel at 5 a.m. every day.
7. News must be regular and reliable.
8. Nayan brought a bottle of fruit juice for the picnic.

abstract nouns

Abstract nouns refer to things which we cannot see or touch but only feel. They include feelings, experiences, states, qualities and ideas.

Examples: Tom was suffering in reality now, so handsomely was his **imagination** working.
You seem to try every way you can to break my old heart with your **outrageousness**.

B. Form abstract nouns from these words from the story. Then fill in the blanks with the suitable words.

ill	think	difficult	discovered	admirable	annoyed

1. The scientist's work led to this important ____________ in the medical field.
2. I have the greatest ____________ for those who help animals.
3. The doctor prescribed three types of medicines for her ____________.
4. I share all my ____________, both happy and sad, with my best friend.
5. The loudspeakers are causing such ____________ to everyone in the area.
6. We found the house without any ____________ because of the host's clear directions.

Study Skills

Pronunciation

long and short *i*

Look at these word pairs and say them aloud.

bit – bite **pin – pine** **win – whine**

The first word in each pair has the short *i* sound, while the second word has the long *i* sound.

Read the words aloud. Write the words with the short *i* sound under *pin* and those with the long *i* sound under *pine*.

pipe time sit flight like shin din dine pick shine

short *i* sound as in *pin*	long *i* sound as in *pine*

Listening

listening for facts

Listen to a passage about a self-made man and fill in the blanks.

1. The narrator's father was ______________ years old when he came from Burma.
2. In Burma, he worked at a ______________ during the day.
3. When he first reached Chennai, he worked at ______________.
4. He never made ______________ to skip work.
5. After that he was appointed as a ______________ in a ______________ office.
6. He wrote small articles for the ______________ section of the paper.
7. One of his articles caught the eye of the ______________ of the newspaper.
8. He retired at the age of ______________.

Dictation

You will now listen to a short passage about Tom Sawyer and write it down. Each sentence will be repeated twice. Listen carefully and be careful not to make any spelling errors.

Speaking

think-pair-share

Work in pairs and think of an incident when you were late to school and had to make up excuses. It can be something interesting or funny. Now narrate the anecdote to the class, speaking for a minute.

Useful words and phrases			
unexpected	fun	disappointed	surprise
anxious	excited	noisy	terrible
hurried	secret	lost	hungry
shout	remove	chalk	scolding
happy	strict	drama	knowledge
ghost	prank	eager	silence
absent	activity	exam	punishment

Writing

informal letter

In the story, Tom realizes that sometimes our mischief may come back to bite us. Imagine that you are Tom. Write a humorous letter to your best friend, Huckleberry Finn, telling him about the incident and the lesson you have learnt.
You may include the following points:

- why you came up with the plan
- the various ailments you thought of
- how you were outsmarted
- feeling embarrassed when caught out

Now I can... Self-Assessment

- o read and enjoy a funny story about the consequences of pretending to be ill.
- o understand and use idioms and colloquialisms.
- o understand and use countable, uncountable, singular, plural and abstract nouns.
- o pronounce words with long *i* and short *i* sounds correctly.
- o narrate an anecdote in pairs, and write an informal letter.

Read at Leisure

The Adventures of Huckleberry Finn: This book by Mark Twain is about the escapades and exciting twists and turns in the life of Tom Sawyer's rebellious friend, Huckleberry Finn.

The Little Prince: This book by Antoine de Saint-Exupery is about a curious young prince from another planet whom the narrator, a pilot, meets in the Sahara Desert, where his aircraft has crashed.

lyric poem

2 Silver

Walter de la Mare

Reading

Have you noticed how the world looks on a bright, full-moon night? Read a poem in which the moon is imagined as a beautiful lady who transforms ordinary things and creatures into objects of beauty as she walks among them.

Literary terms

1. This is an example of **personification**. The moon is imagined as a lady walking around slowly at night.
2. This is an example of **alliteration**, as the /k/ sound is repeated in consecutive words.
3. This is a **simile**. The dog, sleeping soundly, is as motionless as a log.
4. This is a **metaphor**. The peaceful nature of the birds is compared to the peace that sleep provides.

Slowly, silently, now the moon
Walks the night in her silver **shoon**[1];
This way, and that, she **peers**, and sees
Silver fruit upon silver trees;
One by one the **casements** catch[2]
Her beams beneath the silvery **thatch**;
Couched in his kennel, like a log[3],
With paws of silver sleeps the dog;
From their shadowy **cote** the white breasts peep
Of doves in silver feathered sleep[4]
A harvest mouse goes scampering by,
With silver claws, and silver eye;
And moveless fish in the water gleam,
By silver **reeds** in a silver stream.

Where is the dog sleeping?

shoon: (archaic) plural of shoes
peers: looks intently
casements: windows that open by means of hinges
thatch: straw-covered roof
couched: tucked in for sleeping
cote: a small shelter for doves and pigeons
reeds: tall grass-like plants with hollow stems that grow in or near water

About the poet

Walter de la Mare (1873–1956) was a British poet, novelist and writer of short stories. His works are known for their imaginative quality and atmosphere. His poetry collection, *Songs of Childhood* is considered a significant example of children's literature.

Understanding the poem

A. Choose the correct answer.

1. The moon walks the ______________ (path/night/sky).
2. The dog is ______________ (stretched out/barking/couched) inside its kennel.
3. The ______________ (doves/sparrows/pigeons) are inside their cote.
4. The harvest mouse ______________ (rolls/scampers/struts) by.
5. The fish are ______________ (finless/tailless/moveless).

B. Answer the questions with reference to context.

1. *This way, and that, she peers, and sees...*
   a. Who is 'she' here?
   b. What does she see?
   c. What happens to the casements as she passes by them?
2. *From their shadowy cote the white breasts peep...*
   a. What is the 'cote'? Why is it 'shadowy'?
   b. Explain the meaning of the phrase, 'silver-feathered sleep'.
   c. Which other creature is also asleep and how has he been described?

Life Skills and Values — imagination

1. In the poem, all the creatures, except one, are motionless. Name it, and explain what it does and how it looks.
2. In the poem, the moon is imagined as a beautiful lady. Describe in your own words what she does and how it changes an ordinary night into a magical scene.
3. Do you think imagination can help us to see things differently from the way they really are?

Vocabulary

crossword

A. Complete the crossword with words from the poem. The meanings of the words are given as clues.

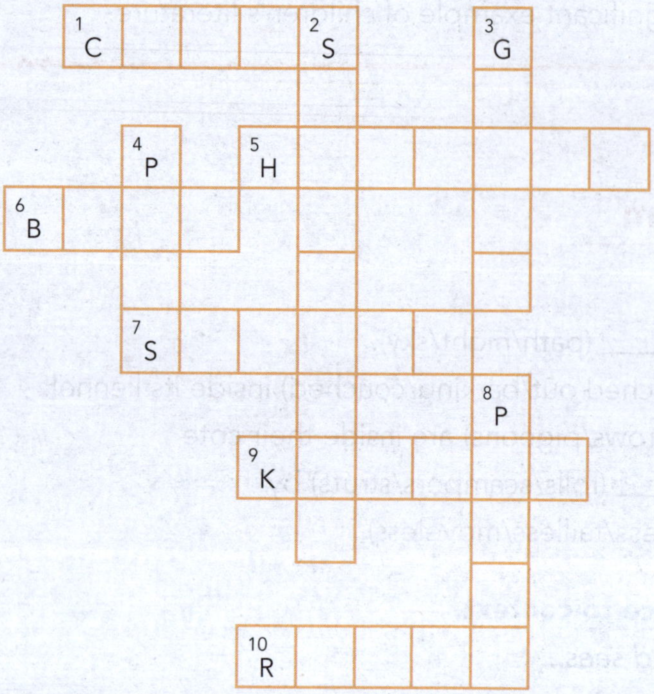

Across

1. curved nails on an animal's foot
5. time for gathering crops
6. ray of light
7. a narrow waterbody
9. a shelter for a dog to sleep in
10. grass that grows in marshy and muddy areas

Down

2. moved quickly with short light steps
3. shine
4. animal feet
8. looks searchingly

suffixes

Look at these words.

move**less** silent**ly**

These words are formed by adding suffixes to the words *move* and *silent*.

Suffixes are groups of letters added after a word to form a new word.

B. Match the words and the suffixes to make new words. Then, fill in the blanks with the words you have made.

colour	comfort	brilliant	magic
bright	free	entertain	decide

-ance	-ness	-ment	-ful
-sion	-al	-dom	-able

1. The king was believed to have __________ powers, with which he could control dragons.
2. Ria tried her best to make the guests feel __________.
3. Children love the __________ walls of the classroom, painted by the teachers themselves.

4. My grandfather was a very strict man. Once he had taken a ________, no one could change his mind.
5. The ________ of the summer sun blinded me for a moment.
6. Romit's ________ shone through in each of his paintings.
7. ________ fighters like Bhagat Singh and Khudiram Bose sacrificed their lives for the country.
8. The radio is the old man's only source of ________.

Activity

speak-a-minute

Imagine that you are a star for one evening, looking down at the world from billions of miles away. Speak in class for one minute, describing the feeling of being at a great height and what you see from your perch in the sky.

Useful words and phrases		
dark night	billions of stars	twinkling
shining	the huge moon	Milky Way
other planets	tiny people on Earth	doing different things

Now I can... — Self-Assessment

- o read and enjoy a poem about the moon.
- o solve a crossword and form new words using suffixes.
- o speak for a minute on a given topic.

Read at Leisure

Who Knows if the Moon's a Balloon: This poem by E. E. Cummings imagines the moon to be a balloon, coming out of a beautiful city in the sky where it is always spring.

One Day I'll Be: This poem by James McDonald is about a child who wants to be an astronaut when he grows up and imagines himself rocketing into space.

II

Quest for Knowledge

Take Off

A. Discuss and answer the following questions in class.

1. Why is education necessary?
2. How does literacy, or the ability to read and write, help us gain knowledge?
3. Can someone be knowledgeable without being able to read and write? Can you think of such a person in real life?
4. Name a noted Indian emperor who could not read or write.

B. Cricket is a very popular game with Indian children. Work in pairs and identify these fielding positions in the game of cricket.

deep   silly point   gully   slip   wicket keeper   mid-wicket

1. The fielder stands close to the batsman and is considered 'silly': _________
2. This player 'keeps' or handles the wicket: _________
3. This fielder stands towards the middle of the wicket: _________
4. This fielder stands close to the wicket keeper to catch the ball slipping away from the bat: _________
5. This fielder is far away or at the deep end of the field: _________
6. This fielder stands on the narrow strip between point and slip: _________

short story

3 How I Taught My Grandmother to Read

Sudha Murty

Reading

Imagine how it would feel if you did not know how to read or write. Not every person is fortunate enough to be able to go to school and receive proper education. Read a story about a grandmother who decided to bring about a change in her situation, despite her age.

When I was a girl of about twelve, I used to stay in a village in north Karnataka with my grandparents. In those days, the transport system was not very good, so we used to get the morning paper only in the afternoon. All of us would wait eagerly for the bus which used to come with the papers, weekly magazines and the post.

At that time, Triveni was a very popular writer in the Kannada language. One of her novels, called *Kashi Yatre*, was appearing as a **serial** in the Kannada weekly, *Karmaveera* at the time.

Food for thought

A pen name is a name used by a writer instead of their real name. This is done either to hide the author's identity or to use a short name which inspires them. Triveni is the pen name of the author, Anasuya Shankar. She wrote about issues faced by women.

My grandmother, Krishtakka, never went to school. So she could not read. Every Wednesday, *Karmaveera* would come and I would read the next episode of *Kashi Yatre* to her. During that time, she would forget all her work and listen with the greatest concentration. Later, she could repeat the entire text by heart. After hearing what happened next in *Kashi Yatre*, she would join her friends at the temple courtyard where the children would also gather to play hide and seek. She would discuss the latest episode with her friends.

Once I went for a wedding with my cousins to the neighbouring village. In those days, a wedding was a great event. We enjoyed ourselves thoroughly. We would eat and play endlessly, **savouring** the freedom because all the elders were busy. I went for a couple of days but ended up staying for a week.

serial: a story on television or the radio, or in a magazine, that is broadcast or published in several separate parts

savouring: enjoying

When I came back to my village, I found my grandmother in tears. I was surprised, for I had never seen her cry even in the most difficult of situations. What had happened? I was worried.

'*Avva,* is everything all right? Are you okay?'

I used to call her *avva*, which means 'mother' in Kannada.

What does the word *avva* mean?

She nodded but did not reply. I did not understand and forgot about it. In the night, after dinner, we were sleeping in the open terrace of the house. It was a summer night and there was a full moon. *Avva* came and sat next to me. Her affectionate hands touched my forehead. I realized she wanted to speak. I asked her, 'What is the matter?'

'When I was a young girl, I lost my mother. There was nobody to look after and guide me. My father was a busy man and got married again. In those days, people never considered education **essential** for girls, so I never went to school. I got married very young and had children. I became very busy. Later, I had grandchildren and always felt so happy cooking and feeding all of you. At times, I used to **regret** not going to school, so I made sure that my children and grandchildren studied well...'

I could not understand why my sixty-two-year-old grandmother was telling me, a twelve-year-old, the story of her life in the middle of the night. But I knew I loved her **immensely** and there had to be some reason why she was talking to me. I looked at her face. It was unhappy and her eyes were filled with tears. She was a good-looking lady who was usually always smiling.

Even today, I cannot forget the worried expression on her face. I leaned forward and held her hand.

'*Avva,* don't cry. What is the matter? Can I help you in any way?'

'Yes, I need your help. You know, when you were away, *Karmaveera* came as usual. I opened the magazine. I saw the picture that **accompanies** the story of *Kashi Yatre* but I could not understand anything that was written. Many times, I rubbed my hands over the pages wishing they could understand what was written. But I knew it was not possible. If only I were educated enough. I waited eagerly for you to return. I felt you would come early and read for me. I even thought of going to the village and asking you to read for me. I could have asked somebody in this village but I was too **embarrassed** to do so. I felt so very dependent and helpless. We are well-off, but what use is money when I cannot be independent?'

I did not know what to answer. *Avva* continued.

'I have decided to learn the Kannada alphabet from tomorrow onwards. I will work very hard. I want to be independent.'

What did *Avva* want to learn from the next day?

essential: very important

regret: feel sad for not having done something

immensely: to a great extent, extremely

accompanies: goes or is carried with something

embarrassed: ashamed

'*Avva,* at this age of sixty-two you want to learn the alphabet? All your hair is grey, your hands are **wrinkled**, you wear spectacles and you work so much in the kitchen...'

But she just smiled.

'For a good cause, if you are determined, you can overcome any **obstacle**. I will work harder than anybody else but I will do it. For learning, age is no limit.'

The next day onwards, I started my **tuition**. *Avva* was a wonderful student. The amount of homework she did was amazing. She would read, repeat, write and recite. I was her only teacher and she was my first student. Little did I know then that one day I would become a teacher of computer science and teach hundreds of students.

Then the *Dussehra* festival came as usual. My grandmother called me to the place of worship and made me sit on a stool. She gave me a gift. It was a length of fabric, to be tailored into a dress. Then she did something unusual. She bent down and touched my feet. I was surprised and taken aback. Elders never touch the feet of youngsters. We only touch the feet of gods we worship, and that of our elders and teachers. We consider it a mark of respect.

She said, 'I am touching the feet of a teacher, not my granddaughter, a teacher who taught me so well and with so much affection that I can now read any novel confidently. Now I am independent.

It is my duty to respect a teacher. Is it not written in our **scriptures** that a teacher should be respected, **irrespective** of age?'

I touched her feet in return and gave my gift to my first student. It was the novel *Kashi Yatre* by Triveni.

I knew then that my student had passed with flying colours[1].

wrinkled: having lines or folds in skin
obstacle: anything that makes it difficult for someone to do something
tuition: teaching
scriptures: holy books
irrespective: without considering something or being influenced by it

Common idioms and proverbs

1. **with flying colours:** This idiom means to do something very well.

About the author

Sudha Murty (born 1950) is an Indian author and educator, and she writes in both Kannada and English. Her stories uphold positive human values like simple living and charity. Some of her well-known works are *The Serpent's Revenge*, *The Day I Stopped Drinking Milk* and *Grandma's Bag of Stories*.

Comprehension

A. Write whether the following statements are true (T) or false (F). Correct the false statements.

1. Triveni was a popular writer in the Telugu language.
2. The narrator's grandmother's name was Krishtakka.
3. *Kashi Yatre* was the name of the Kannada weekly that the narrator's grandmother used to wait for.
4. The narrator went to her cousin's wedding.
5. The narrator's grandmother regretted not going to school.
6. The narrator's grandmother gave her a gift on her birthday.
7. The narrator knew that her teacher had passed with flying colours.

B. Answer the questions.

1. What did the grandmother discuss with her friends at the temple courtyard?
2. Why was a wedding an event of merriment for the children?
3. Why was the narrator's grandmother sad? What did she say about her past?
4. What kind of help did the narrator's grandmother ask for? What was the narrator's reaction to it?
5. Describe how the lessons between the narrator and her grandmother progressed.
6. How did they celebrate *Dussehra* that year?
7. What, according to the grandmother, was written in the scriptures?

C. Answer the questions with reference to context.

1. *Then she did something unusual.*
   a. Who was 'she'? How old was 'she'?
   b. What unusual thing did 'she' do and why?
   c. What did the narrator do then?

Life Skills and Values compassion, right to education

1. What kind of relationship did the narrator share with her grandmother? Explain using lines from the text.
2. Do you agree with Krishtakka's statement that 'For learning, age is no limit'? Explain using lines from the text.

Vocabulary

words related to books and reading

A. Fill in the blanks with the given words related to books and reading.

bookworm author novels avid binding published plot browse

1. Pritam is an ____________ reader of adventure stories.
2. This book has been ____________ in over forty languages.
3. My grandfather is the proud owner of old and rare books in leather ____________.
4. J. K. Rowling is my favourite ____________. I've read all her books.
5. I like to ____________ through the humour section whenever I'm in a bookstore.
6. Divya is such a ____________. She does not go anywhere without a book.
7. My brother loves to read mystery ____________.
8. She has read the story so many times that she knows the ____________ by heart.

forming antonyms with prefixes *dis-*, *un-*, *il-*

We can form antonyms or opposites by adding prefixes like *dis-*, *un-*, *il-* before words.

Examples: She was ***un*happy** and her eyes were filled with tears.
She did not want to ***dis*respect** her teacher.

B. Fill in the blanks with the antonyms of the given words. Add the prefixes *dis-*, *un-*, *-il* to form the antonyms.

1. Sahil's room is big but ____________ (tidy).
2. It does not pay to be ____________ (honest).
3. ____________ (legal) acts are punishable by law.
4. The magician ____________ (appeared) in the blink of an eye.
5. I can't read these notes. The handwriting is ____________ (legible)!
6. This trek route feels quite ____________ (safe).
7. The comics you are looking for have been ____________ (continued).
8. The team tried to win the match by resorting to ____________ (fair) tactics.

Grammar

You know that adjectives describe nouns or pronouns by giving some information about a person's or an object's size, shape, age, colour, origin or material. They are of four main types.

Adjectives of quality describe the quality of a noun, its shape, size, colour, state or condition. They answer the question *what kind of*.

Example: Triveni was a **popular** writer.

Adjectives of quantity specify the quantity of the noun being talked about. They answer the questions *how many/how much*. Some adjectives of quantity are *much, many, little, less, few, a few, a lot*.

Example: **Many** times, I rubbed my hands over the pages.

Demonstrative adjectives are used to point out a specific noun. The four demonstrative adjectives are *this, that, these* and *those*.

Example: In **those** days, people never considered education essential for girls.

Interrogative adjectives are used to ask questions and are always followed by a noun. These are *which, what* and *whose*.

Example: **Which** book did grandmother want to read?

A. Fill in the blanks with the correct adjectives and state their types.

1. I like to eat __________ (many/dark) chocolate.
2. __________ (These/That) books are new.
3. We did not get __________ (less/much) rainfall this year.
4. __________ (That/Which) team are you supporting?
5. The red handbag is __________ (good/better) than the blue one.
6. __________ (This/Which) book have you read recently?
7. There is __________ (enough/most) food for everyone in the fridge.
8. She has __________ (many/great) love for animals.
9. __________ (A few/Whose) passes might be left yet for the concert.

Read these sentences.

She was **my first student**.
I looked **at her face**.

The words *my first student* and *at her face* give additional information about the sentences, but they do not make complete sense on their own. These are known as phrases.

A **phrase** is a group of words which conveys some meaning but does not make complete sense. A phrase does not have a finite verb or a subject of its own.

Now look at this sentence.

I saw the picture that accompanied the story.

Here, the underlined part *I saw the picture* has the subject *I* and the finite verb *saw*. It is a clause.

A **clause** is a group of words that has a subject and a finite verb.

A clause can be a part of the sentence or a sentence by itself.
Example: We waited for the bus **which came with the papers**.

In this sentence, the underlined part *we waited for the bus* is a **main clause** because it has the subject *we*, the finite verb *waited*, and makes complete sense by itself. The part *which came with the papers* is a **subordinate clause** because though it has the finite verb *came*, it depends on the rest of the sentence to make complete sense.

B. Write whether the underlined words are phrases or clauses. In case of a clause, mention whether it is a main or a subordinate clause.

1. Piu bought a puppy from a friend.
2. We all ran into the garden when we saw the butterflies.
3. We left Manali before the snowfall began.
4. I will meet you in front of the playground.
5. It's sad that our favourite teacher is leaving the school.
6. She saw her cat a minute ago.
7. I couldn't invite Ved for the party, because he was not at home.
8. My mother found her misplaced purse.

Study Skills

Dictionary Skills

synonyms

You know that you can use your dictionary to find synonyms of different words.
Examples: selfless: unselfish, generous
dedication: devotion, commitment

Look in your dictionary and choose the correct synonym for each of the given words.

1. handwriting:	____________	a. scrawl	b. screech	c. scratch
2. wrinkled:	____________	a. twinkled	b. winked	c. creased
3. essential:	____________	a. necessary	b. useless	c. sensible
4. obstacle:	____________	a. advantage	b. spectacle	c. difficulty
5. respect:	____________	a. regard	b. inspect	c. disregard
6. thoroughly:	____________	a. loudly	b. wholly	c. roughly

Listening

listening for details

Listen to a passage about a woman's recollections about her grandmother, and fill in the blanks.

1. The grandmother was ____________ and could read ____________ and ____________.
2. The narrator's grandparents used to read a newspaper called ____________.
3. The narrator went to India when she was ____________ years old.
4. The grandmother asked her to write a ____________ to her uncle.
5. The narrator's uncle's hometown was in ____________.
6. The granddaughter used to call her grandmother ____________.
7. The narrator learnt that one should always be ____________.
8. The narrator is now ____________ years old.

Speaking

group discussion

Teaching or educating people is a way of serving the community. How can we help people around us, especially those who are less privileged? In groups of four, think of two ways in which you can serve the community. Then, take turns to share your ideas in class, explaining how they will make a difference.
You can consider the following points:

- People: volunteering at a senior citizens' home, animal shelter, or orphanage
- Environment: raising awareness, organizing clean-up drives
- Helping out at home: reaching out to helpers, the elderly and the weak

Writing

Imagine that you are the narrator of the story and write a short message to your grandmother, telling her that you have gone out to buy a novel by Triveni from the local bookseller. Keep the message short and clear and check that it has these points.

- the heading 'message'
- date, followed by time
- name of the person the message is meant for
- name of the person who writes the message

Now I can... — Self-Assessment

- o read and appreciate a story about the relationship between a grandmother and her granddaughter.
- o use words related to books and reading, and form antonyms using prefixes.
- o use the various types of adjectives, and identify phrases and clauses in sentences.
- o use the dictionary to find synonyms.
- o have a group discussion on a given topic, and write a message.

Read at Leisure

Fablehaven: This series by Brandon Mull is about the adventures of siblings Seth and Kendra in Fablehaven, a protected area for magical creatures, plotting witches, and greedy trolls, whose caretaker is none other than their own grandfather.

Anne of Avonlea: This book by L. M. Montgomery is the second in the *Anne Shirley* series. It describes Anne's new life as a teacher in her old school, as she settles into Avonlea society.

non-fiction

4 Children of India

Ruskin Bond

Reading

How do you go to school—by bus, car, auto or on foot? There are many children in our country who overcome various obstacles daily to reach their schools. Read on to find out how they deal with such adverse situations and come out winners.

They pass me every day, on their way to school – boys and girls from the surrounding villages and the **outskirts** of the hill station. There are no school buses **plying** for these children. For many of them, it's a very long walk to school.

Ranbir, who is ten, has to climb the mountain from his village, four miles distant and two thousand feet below the town level. He comes in all weathers, wearing the same pair of cheap shoes until they have almost fallen apart.

How far is Ranbir's village from the school?

Ranbir is a cheerful soul. He waves to me whenever he sees me at my window. Sometimes he brings cucumbers from his father's field. I pay him for the cucumbers; he uses the money for books or for small things needed at home.

Many of the children are like Ranbir – poor, but slightly better off than what their parents were at the same age. They cannot attend the expensive residential and private schools that **abound** here, but most go to the government-aided schools with only basic facilities. Not many of their parents managed to go to school. They spent their lives working in the fields or delivering milk in the hill station. The lucky ones got into the army. Perhaps Ranbir will do something different when he grows up. He has yet to see a train but he sees planes flying over the mountains almost every day.

'How far can a plane go?' he asks.

'All over the world,' I tell him. 'Thousands of miles in a day. You can go almost anywhere.'

'I'll go round the world one day,' he vows. 'I'll buy a plane and go everywhere!'

outskirts: the parts of a town or city that are farthest from the centre

plying: travelling regularly on a particular route

abound: exist in great numbers

defiant: bold, aggressive

And maybe he will. He has a determined chin and a **defiant** look in his eye. These lines in my journal were put down for my own inspiration or encouragement, but they will do for any determined young person. We get out of life what we bring to it. There is not a dream which may not come true if we have the energy which determines our own fate. We can always get what we want if we will it intensely enough… it may come when we no longer have any use of it, but if we have been willing it long enough, it will come!

Food for thought

Winters are severe in the hills, with heavy snowfall making it impossible for people to come out of their homes for several days. They not only have to store enough food for themselves but also for their animals. They usually do this before winter, when plants have not dried up yet.

Up to a few years ago, very few girls in the hills or in the villages of India went to school. They helped in the home until they were old enough to be married, which wasn't very old. But there are now just as many girls as there are boys going to school.

Bindra is something of an **extrovert**, a confident fourteen-year-old who **chatters away** as she hurries down the road with her companions. Her father is a forest guard and knows me quite well: I meet him on my walks through the *deodar* woods behind Landour. And I had grown used to seeing Bindra almost every day. When she did not put in an appearance[1] for a week, I asked her brother if anything was wrong.

Common idioms and proverbs

1. **put in an appearance:** This idiom means to visit or appear at some place for some time.

'Oh, nothing,' he says, 'she is helping my mother cut grass. Soon the monsoon will end and the grass will dry up. So we cut it now and store it for the cows in winter.'

'And why aren't you cutting grass too?'

'Oh, I have a cricket match today,' he says, and hurries away to join his teammates. Unlike his sister, he puts pleasure before work!

Cricket, once the game of the **elite**, has become the game of the **masses**. On any holiday, in any part of this vast country, groups of boys can be seen working their way to the nearest field, or open patch of land, with bat, ball and any other cricketing **gear** that they can **cobble together**. Watching some of them play, I am amazed at the quality of talent, at the **finesse** with which they bat or bowl.

Some of the local teams are as good, if not better, than any from the private schools, where there are better facilities. But the boys from these

extrovert: a lively and confident person who enjoys being with others

chatters away: talks quickly and continuously

elite: a small group of people in a society who are powerful and have a lot of influence

masses: the ordinary people

gear: the equipment or clothing needed for a particular activity

cobble together: to produce something quickly and without great care or effort, so that it can be used, but is not perfect

finesse: great skill

poor or lower middle-class families will never get the exposure that is necessary to bring them to the attention of those who select state or national teams. They will never get near enough to the men of influence and power. They must continue to play for the love of[2] the game, to watch their more fortunate heroes' **exploits** on television.

As winter approaches and the days grow shorter, those children who live far away must **quicken** their pace in order to get home before dark. Ranbir and his friends find that darkness has fallen before they are half way home.

Common idioms and proverbs

2. **for the love of:** This idiom means for the sake of something.

'What is the time, Uncle?' he asks, as he **trudges** up the **steep** road past *Ivy Cottage*. One gets used to being called 'Uncle' by almost every boy or girl one meets. I wonder how the custom began. Perhaps it has its origins in the folktale about the tiger who **refrained** from **pouncing** on you if you called him 'Uncle'. Tigers don't eat their relatives! Or do they? The ploy may not work if the tiger happens to be a tigress. Would you call her 'Aunty' as she (or your teacher!) descends on you?

It's dark at six and by then, Ranbir likes to be out of the *deodar* forest and on the open road to the village. The moon and the stars and the village lights are sufficient, but not in the forest, where it is dark even during the day. And the silent **flitting** of bats and **flying foxes**[3], and the **eerie** hoot of an owl, can be a little **disconcerting** for the **hardiest** of children. Once Ranbir and the other boys were chased by a bear.

Literary term

3. This is an example of **alliteration**, as the 'f' sound is repeated in consecutive words.

When he told me about it, I said, 'Well, now we know you can run faster than a bear!'

'Yes, but you have to run downhill when chased by a bear.' He spoke as one having long experience of escaping from bears. 'They run much faster uphill!'

'I'll remember that,' I said, 'thanks for the advice.' And I don't suppose calling a bear 'Uncle' would help.

Usually Ranbir has the company of other boys, and they sing most of the way, for loud singing by small boys will silence owls and frighten away

What music can be heard in the mountains?

exploits: brave, exciting or interesting acts
trudges: walks slowly with heavy steps
steep: sharply rising, not gradual
refrained: stopped oneself from doing something
pouncing: moving suddenly forwards to attack
flitting: swift and light movement
flying foxes: large fruit bats
eerie: strange and frightening
disconcerting: feeling unsettled and anxious
hardiest: the strongest and most resourceful

the forest demons. One of them plays a flute, and flute music in the mountains is always enchanting.

Not only in the hills, but all over India, children are constantly making their way to and from school, in conditions that range from dust storms in the Rajasthan desert to **blizzards** in Ladakh and Kashmir. In the larger towns and cities, there are school buses, but in **remote** rural areas, getting to school can pose a problem.

Most children are more than equal to any obstacles that may arise. Like those youngsters in the Ganjam district of Orissa. In the absence of a bridge, they swim or **wade** across the Dhanei river every day in order to reach their school. I have a picture of them in my scrapbook. Holding books or **satchels aloft** in one hand, they do the breast stroke or dog paddle with the other; or form a chain and help each other across.

Wherever you go in India, you will find children helping out with the family's source of livelihood, whether it be drying fish on the Malabar Coast, or gathering saffron buds in Kashmir, or grazing camels or cattle in a village in Rajasthan or Gujarat. Only the more fortunate can afford to send their children to English medium private or 'public schools', and those children really *are* fortunate, for some of these institutions are excellent schools, as good, and often better, than their **counterparts** in Britain or the USA. Whether it's in Ajmer or Bangalore, New Delhi or Chandigarh, Kanpur or Calcutta, the best schools set very high standards.

The great majority of our children will attend schools run by the state or municipality. These vary from good to the bad to the ugly, depending on how they are run and where they are situated.

A classroom without windows, or with a roof that lets in the monsoon rain, is not uncommon. Even so, children from different communities learn to live and grow together. Hardship makes brothers of us all.

The **census** tells us that two in every five of the population is in the age group of five to fifteen. Almost half our population is on the way to school!

And here I stand at my window, watching some of them pass by – boys and girls, big and small, some **scruffy**, some smart, some mischievous, some serious, but all *going* somewhere – hopefully towards a better future.

blizzards: snowstorms with very strong winds
remote: isolated, far away from places where people live
wade: walk with an effort through water or mud
satchels: bags carried on the shoulder by long straps and closed by a flap
aloft: high in the air
counterparts: people or things identical to or closely resembling another
census: an official count of the population
scruffy: shabby and untidy

About the author

Ruskin Bond (born 1934) is an Indian author of British origin. He has written many books for children as well as adults. He is best-known for his short stories set in Himalayan towns. Some of his most-loved stories are *The Blue Umbrella*, *Harold the Hornbill* and *Tiger in the Tunnel*.

Comprehension

A. Read the sentences in each set and tick (✓) the ones that are correct.

1. a. Ranbir brought cabbages for the author. ☐
   b. Ranbir brought cucumbers for the author. ☐
   c. Ranbir brought apples for the author. ☐
2. a. The lucky ones got jobs in multinational companies. ☐
   b. The lucky ones got into hospitals. ☐
   c. The lucky ones got into the army. ☐
3. a. Bindra's father was a school guard. ☐
   b. Bindra's father was a forest guard. ☐
   c. Bindra's father was a shopkeeper. ☐
4. a. Cricket, once the game of the elite, has become the game of the masses. ☐
   b. Cricket, once the game of the masses, has become the game of the elite. ☐
   c. Cricket, once the game of the children, has become the game of the adults. ☐
5. a. The tiger should be called 'father' for it to not attack someone. ☐
   b. The tiger should be called 'uncle' for it to not attack someone. ☐
   c. The tigress should be called 'uncle' for it to not attack someone. ☐
6. a. The great majority of our children will attend English medium private schools. ☐
   b. The great majority of our children will attend boarding schools. ☐
   c. The great majority of our children will attend schools run by the state or municipality. ☐

B. Answer the questions with reference to context.

1. *'I'll go round the world one day,' he vows.*
   a. Who said these words and to whom?
   b. Why did he say this and how did he plan to achieve this?
   c. What is said about his appearance?
   d. How does he come across as determined while going to school?

2. *'She is helping my mother cut grass.'*
   a. Who said these words? Who was 'she'?
   b. Why was she helping her mother to cut grass? What did she miss out on for doing this?
   c. Did the speaker help in the work too? What opinion did the author form of him?

3. *'Well, now we know you can run faster than a bear!'*
   a. Who could run faster than a bear?
   b. Why did he have to do so?
   c. Where was he when this incident took place? What advice did he give the author?
   d. How did the boys ensure their safety?

4. *Most children are more than equal to any obstacles that may arise.*
   a. In what conditions do children in Rajasthan, Ladakh and Kashmir make their way to and from school?
   b. What picture does the author have in his scrapbook? Describe how the children depicted in the picture overcome their obstacle.
   c. How do the children from the Malabar Coast and Kashmir help their family earn a livelihood?

Life Skills and Values — gender equality, love for sport

1. What do you think of the difference in treatment between Bindra and her brother with regard to balancing chores, studies and play?
2. 'Hardship makes brothers of us all.' Do you agree with the author? Explain your answer with examples from the passage.
3. What does the author feel about the popularity of cricket in India? Why does he say that the boys in the hills must continue to play for the love of the game, and not for any gains or glories?

Vocabulary

commonly confused words

A. Choose the correct words to complete the sentences.

1. This dress is a little ____________ (lose/loose) for me.
2. I ran into Hema's ____________ (elder/older) brother at the mall.
3. My father ____________ (ensured/insured) our new car against any kind of accident.
4. Please ____________ (accept/except) the invitation to the opening night of the play.
5. The trekkers returned midway because of ____________ (averse/adverse) weather conditions.
6. After the three-course meal, we still had room for ____________ (desert/dessert).

B. Several phrasal verbs like *got into* and *help out* have been used in the passage. Fill in the blanks with the correct options.

put up | fell apart | get into | gave up | put in | put down | passed by

1. He ______________ his thoughts and ideas in a secret diary.
2. Roy ______________ his position as the captain of the football team after they lost the final game.
3. Their friendship ______________ over a petty quarrel.
4. I cannot ______________ this dress, it seems to have shrunk.
5. The actor's convoy ______________ our house today.
6. All the children ______________ splendid performances.
7. She ______________ with all the nuisance created by the puppy.

Grammar

subject and predicate

Read these sentences.

Ranbir *is a cheerful soul.*

Most children *are more than equal to any obstacles that may arise.*

A sentence has two parts — a subject and a predicate. Here, the underlined words, *Ranbir* and *Most children* are the subjects and the remaining parts of the sentences are the predicates.

The **subject** tells us who or what the sentence is about. The **predicate** has a verb and tells us something about the subject. To identify the subject in a sentence, we find the verb and then ask *who* or *what* does the action.

A. Circle the subjects and underline the predicates in the sentences.

1. Rohan is a bright and cheerful boy.
2. My sister has two pet rabbits.
3. Tigers are endangered animals.
4. Parul and her brother are both swimming champions.
5. I met my cousins recently.
6. My parents are talking to the guests.
7. This library has a vast collection of old and rare books.
8. We want to play a game of hide-and-seek now.

You know that tenses cover three aspects of time—the past, the present and the future. Each tense can be categorised into further types.

The **simple present tense** is used to talk about things that happen regularly or are universal truths.

Example: They pass me every day on their way to school.

The **present continuous tense** is used to describe a continuous or an ongoing action in the present time.

Example: She is helping my mother cut grass.

The **simple past tense** is used to refer to actions that were completed before the time of speaking.

Example: I asked her brother if anything was wrong.

The **past continuous tense** is used to talk about actions that went on for some time in the past.

Example: Ranbir was wearing the same pair of cheap shoes.

The **simple future tense** is used for actions that will happen at some point of time in the future.

Example: I will buy a plane and go everywhere.

The **future continuous tense** is used for actions that will start in the future and continue for some time.

Example: Soon the monsoon will be ending.

B. Underline the verbs and identify their tense.

1. The train will arrive at 8 p.m.
2. The little girl is playing with the puppy.
3. Mohit returned the book to the library yesterday.
4. The trees look lovely in autumn with red and golden leaves.
5. They were enjoying the meal served at the restaurant.
6. We will be spending our holidays in Darjeeling this year.

C. Complete the sentences using the correct form of the given verbs.

1. He ______________ (participate) in the Olympiad next month.
2. I ______________ (visit) my grandmother last week.
3. The teacher ______________ (check) our assignments now.
4. By this time next year, I ______________ (study) in the seventh standard.

5. Tarun ______________ (go) to the book market on Sundays.
6. Jane ______________ (wait) for the bus when the rain started.

Study Skills

Spelling

names of professions using *-er, -ian, -ist*

Look at these words.

cricket**er** musici**an** journal**ist**

These are names of professions formed by adding suffixes like *-er*, *-ian* and *-ist* to the base words *cricket*, *music* and *journal* respectively.

Fill in the blanks with suitable names of professions.

1. The ______________ painted the doors and windows white.
2. The ______________ thrilled the audience with his disappearing tricks.
3. We had to call the ______________ to replace the bulbs and lights.
4. The ______________ has discovered a cure for the deadly disease.
5. The ______________ had a barn full of cattle and horses.
6. The art exhibition was inaugurated by a famous ______________.

Listening

listening for information

Listen to a passage about volunteering at a wildlife sanctuary. Then write whether the following statements are true (T) or false (F).

1. The narrator worked at a wildlife sanctuary in South America. ☐
2. More than a hundred animals lived there. ☐
3. The narrator once had breakfast while a baboon sat next to her. ☐
4. Lions and leopards roamed freely in the sanctuary. ☐
5. The cheetahs had been rescued as orphans. ☐
6. The narrator used to observe elephants and rhinoceroses in the wild. ☐
7. The narrator enjoyed bathing the baby animals the most. ☐
8. There were meerkats, mongooses, porcupines, tortoises, and deer. ☐

Speaking

participating in a debate

Social media has replaced books and reading as a source of information and enjoyment. Do you agree? Work in two groups and have a debate in class on the topic, one group speaking for the motion and the other against it.

Useful words and phrases

I believe/feel that...

I do not quite agree with...

I should point out that...

Writing

writing essays

A narrative essay usually describes an event and has plenty of action. A descriptive essay is a detail-rich account of a scene or event. Write two essays about a cricket match, one in the narrative style and one in the descriptive style.
You can use the following points:

Descriptive style

- sights, tastes, sounds and smells of a stadium
- weather and pitch conditions
- details about the players, their uniforms, expressions

Narrative style

- who won the toss, how the match progressed
- memorable moments, the crowd's reactions
- feelings and experiences of the spectators

Now I can... **Self-Assessment**

- o read and learn about the obstacles Indian children overcome in their pursuit of education.
- o use commonly confused words and phrasal verbs.
- o identify subject and predicate and use the different types of tenses in sentences.
- o participate in a debate on a given topic.
- o write essays, both from the descriptive and the narrative approach.

Read at Leisure

Oliver Twist: This book by Charles Dickens is the story of an orphan boy in various adverse conditions, whose determination helps him to survive against all odds.

I am Malala: This memoir by Malala Yousafzai is the story of young girl who refused to be silenced and fought for her right to an education.

III

Humour

Take Off

A. Here are some famous people or fictional characters who never fail to make us laugh. Match their pictures with their descriptions and name them.

1. His character, *The Tramp* has been loved since the silent-film era. His trademark look consisted of white face paint, bowler hat, and toothbrush moustache. Some of his famous films are *The Kid*, *The Gold Rush* and *City Lights*.

2. He was an English author, poet and illustrator, famous for his humorous limericks. Most of his limericks start with 'There was an old lady/man of...', and go on to describe strange scenarios.

3. They were a pair of comedians, one of them rake-thin, and the other, the complete opposite. They acted in many comic films together, wearing bowler hats, and doing clumsy and childish things.

4. He is a clumsy man who goes about causing trouble even as he tries to perform simple, everyday tasks. He is instantly recognized by his bulging eyes and silly smile. He appears in multiple TV shows.

5. They are a working class American family who are the subject of one of the longest running animated TV shows. They deal with situations in life in a comical way, and often get their eccentric neighbours, friends and relatives involved as well.

a. 

b. 

c. 

d. 

e. 

B. A style of music is often referred to as a *genre*. The names of some music genres followed in India are given in the box. Discuss in class and match them with their descriptions.

rap	bhajan	bhangra	folk music	pop music	qawwali

1. a style of music with a strong rhythm and simple tunes, popular since the 1950s: ______________
2. a type of Punjabi dance music with instrumental beats: ______________
3. traditional music of the native people of a place, like *Baul* (Bengal), *Garba* (Gujarat): __________
4. fast-paced Sufi music: ______________
5. Hindu devotional music: ______________
6. a type of music where words are recited rapidly and in rhythm: ______________

(The answers are given at the end of the chapter.)

5 A Hero

R. K. Narayan

Reading

Are you afraid of the dark? Do you sleep alone at night? Read this story to find out what happened when a ten-year-old boy was asked to sleep alone in a dark room at night.

Father looked over the newspaper he was reading and said, 'Swami, listen to this: "News is **at hand** of the bravery of a village lad who, while returning home by the jungle path, came **face to face** with a tiger..."' The paragraph described the fight the boy had with the tiger and his **flight up** a tree, where he stayed for half a day till some people came that way and rescued him.

After reading it through, Father looked at Swaminathan and asked, 'What do you say to that?'

Swaminathan said, 'I think he must have been a very strong and grown-up person, not at all a boy. How could a boy fight a tiger?'

Food for thought

R. K. Narayan set most of his stories in the imaginary town of Malgudi in south India. Many of the stories are about a ten-year-old boy named Swami, and his friends. Though Malgudi is a fictional city, it is believed to have been based on Malleswaram and Basavanagudi, two localities in Bangalore that the author was familiar with.

'You think you are wiser than the newspaper?' Father **sneered**. 'A man may have the strength of an elephant and yet be a coward: whereas another may have the strength of a straw, but if he has courage, he can do anything.'

Swami **disputed** the theory. 'How can it be, Father? Suppose I have all the courage, what can I do if a tiger should attack me?'

What theory did Swami disagree with?

'Leave alone strength, can you prove you have courage? Let me see if you can sleep alone tonight in my office room.'

A frightful idea, Swaminathan thought. He had always slept beside his Granny, and any change in this arrangement kept him trembling and awake all night.

at hand: close by
face to face: facing each other
flight up: climb up
sneered: curled the upper lip to show lack of respect
disputed: disagreed

He hoped that his father was only joking. He mumbled weakly, 'Yes,' and tried to change the subject.

Then he said, 'From the first of next month I'll sleep alone, Father.'

'No, you must do it now. It is **disgraceful** sleeping beside Granny or Mother. You are in the Second Form now,' he said, and looked at his wife, who was rocking the cradle.

'Why do you look at me while you say it?' she asked. 'I hardly know anything about the boy.'

Food for thought

The term 'Second Form' refers to the seventh standard. In British India, classes in secondary school started from the first form (Class VI) and went up to the sixth form (Class XI).

Swaminathan rose silently and tiptoed away to his bed in the passage. Granny was sitting up in her bed, and remarked, 'Boy, are you already feeling sleepy? Don't you want a story?' Swaminathan made wild **gesticulations** to silence his Granny, but that good lady saw nothing.

How do we know that Swami had a sibling?

Swaminathan threw himself on his bed and pulled the blanket over his face.

Granny said, 'Don't cover your face. Are you really very sleepy?'

Swaminathan leant over and whispered, 'Please, please, Granny, don't talk to me, and don't let anyone call me even if the house is on fire. If I don't sleep at once I shall perhaps die.'

He turned over, curled, and began snoring under the blanket till he found his blanket pulled away.

'Swami, get up,' Father said.

Swaminathan stirred and groaned as if in sleep. Granny pleaded, 'Why do you disturb him?'

'Get up, Swami,' he said again and Swaminathan got up. Father rolled up his bed, took it under his arm, and said, 'Come with me.'

Swaminathan looked at his Granny, hesitated for a moment, and followed his father into the office room. On the way, he threw a look of **appeal** at his mother.

She said, 'Why do you take him to the office room? He can sleep in the hall.'

'I don't think so,' Father said, and Swaminathan **slunk** behind him with bowed head.

'Let me sleep in the hall, Father,' he pleaded. 'Your office room is very dusty and there may be scorpions behind your law books.'

'There are no scorpions, little fellow. Sleep on the bench if you like.'

'Can I have a lamp burning in the room?'

'No. You must learn not to be afraid of darkness. It is only a question of habit.'

'Will you at least leave the door open?'

'All right. But promise you will not roll up your bed and go to your Granny's side at night. If you do it, mind you, I will tell everyone in your school.'

Swaminathan felt cut off from humanity. He was pained and angry. He didn't like the **strain** of cruelty he saw in his father's nature. He hated the newspaper for printing the tiger's story. He wished that the tiger hadn't spared the boy, who didn't appear to be a boy after all, but a monster.

disgraceful: very bad or unacceptable

gesticulations: movements done by hands and arms to attract attention or make somebody understand what one is saying

appeal: heartfelt request

slunk: moved away in fear

strain: a particular quality in the character of a person

As the night progressed, his heart beat faster. He remembered all the stories of devils and ghosts he had heard in his life. How often had Mani seen the devil in the banyan tree at his street end? And what about poor Munisami's father, who spat out blood because the devil near the river's edge slapped his cheek when he was returning home late one night? He was **faint** with fear. A ray of light from the street lamp strayed in and cast shadows on the wall. He covered himself so completely that he could hardly breathe. Every moment he expected the devils to come up to carry him away.

Swaminathan hurriedly got up and spread his bed under the bench and crouched there. It seemed to be a much safer place, more compact and reassuring. He shut his eyes tight and **encased** himself in his blanket once again and unknown to himself, fell asleep, and was racked with nightmares[1].

A tiger was chasing him. His feet stuck to the ground. He desperately tried to escape but his feet would not move; the tiger was at his back, and he could hear its claws scratch the ground ... scratch, scratch, and then a light thud ...

Swaminathan tried to open his eyes, but his eyelids would not open and the nightmare continued. Swaminathan groaned, and with a desperate effort he opened his eyes. He put his hand out to feel his Granny's presence at his side, as was his habit, but he only touched the wooden leg of the bench. His lonely state came back to him. He sweated with fright.

Common idioms and proverbs

1. **racked with nightmares:** This idiom refers to the distress caused by nightmares. *Racked with* can also be used with the words *fear* or *guilt*.

And now what was this **rustling**? Something was moving down. He lay gazing at it in horror. His end had come. He realized that the devil would presently pull him out and tear him apart, and so why should he wait? As it came nearer, he crawled out from under the bench, hugged it with all his **might**, and used his teeth on it like a **mortal** weapon.

'*Aiyo!* Something has bitten me,' went **forth** an **agonized**, thundering cry and was followed by a heavy tumbling and falling amidst furniture.

faint: feeling weak
encased: covered
rustling: a low rubbing sound made by dry leaves or paper
might: great strength
mortal: deadly
forth: out
agonized: expressing severe pain

In a moment Father, the cook and a servant came in, carrying lights. And all three of them fell on the burglar who lay amidst the furniture with a bleeding ankle...

Congratulations were showered on Swaminathan the next day. His classmates looked at him with respect, and his teacher patted his back. The Headmaster said that he was a true **scout**. Swaminathan had bitten into the flesh of one of the most **notorious** housebreakers of the district and the police were grateful to him for it.

The Inspector said, 'Why don't you join the police when you grow up?'

Swaminathan said for the sake of politeness, 'Certainly, yes,' though he had quite made up his mind to be an engine driver, a railway guard or a bus conductor later in life.

When he returned home that night, Father asked, 'Where is the boy?'

'He is asleep. He didn't have a wink of sleep the whole of last night,' said his mother.

'Where is he sleeping?'

'In his usual place,' Mother said casually. 'He went to bed at seven-thirty.'

'Sleeping beside his Granny again!' Father said. 'No wonder he wanted to be asleep before I could return home.'

When did Swaminathan go to bed that night?

Mother lost her temper. 'You let him sleep where he likes. You needn't risk his life again.'

Father mumbled, 'Alright, **mollycoddle** him as much as you like. But don't blame me afterwards.'

Swaminathan felt tremendously relieved to hear that his father was giving up on him.

scout: a boy or girl who is a member of a worldwide organization which teaches them to be practical, sensible, and helpful

notorious: known to everyone for being bad

mollycoddle: pamper somebody too much

About the author

R. K. Narayan (1906–2001) was one of the most celebrated writers of Indian literature in English. He wrote about the everyday lives of ordinary people with humour and kindness. One of his best-known works is *Swami and His Friends*, set in the fictional town of Malgudi. He received the Sahitya Akademi Award for his book, *Guide*, which was also made into a film.

Comprehension

A. Choose the correct answer.

1. The newspaper described the fight the boy had with the ______________.
   a. bear b. tiger c. elephant
2. Swaminathan's father asked him to sleep in the ______________.
   a. hall b. bedroom c. office room
3. According to his father, Swami had to learn not to be afraid of ______________.
   a. darkness b. scorpions c. ghosts
4. In Swami's nightmare, a ______________ was chasing him.
   a. tiger b. devil c. burglar

5. The Headmaster called Swami a true ___________.
   a. hero b. scout c. coward
6. Swami had made up his mind to be a ___________ in future.
   a. railway guard b. housebreaker c. lawyer
7. After the incident, Swami went back to sleeping with his ___________.
   a. mother b. father c. grandmother

B. Complete this character study of Swami's father, by filling in the character traits and supporting lines from the text.

Character traits	Lines from the text
1. He was a strict father.	a.
2.	b. 'You think you are wiser than the newspaper?'
3.	c. 'There are no scorpions, little fellow. Sleep on the bench if you like'.
4.	d. 'Get up, Swami,' he said again and Swaminathan got up. Father rolled up his bed, took it under his arm, and said, 'Come with me.'
5. He was quite short-tempered.	e.
6.	f. In a moment Father, the cook and a servant came in, carrying lights.

C. Answer the questions with reference to context.

1. *'Will you leave the door open?'*
   a. Who said these words and to whom?
   b. Why did the speaker ask this question? Did the person spoken to agree to his request? On what condition did he agree to it?
   c. What was the speaker reminded of later in the night?
2. *He realised that the devil would presently pull him out and tear him apart, so why should he wait.*
   a. Who is 'he' here? What made him think that the devil had come for him?
   b. What did 'he' do as it came nearer to him? Was it actually a devil?
   c. What happened immediately afterwards?

Life Skills and Values — humour, overcoming fear

1. Did you find the story humorous? Give some examples from the story.
2. Why did the thought of sleeping alone bring out so many fears in Swami?
3. Should we mock another's difficulties or fears? Think of the situations in the story and answer.
4. Was Swami's father 'cruel'? Why was he insisting on Swami sleeping in the office by himself?

Vocabulary

contextual usage

A. Rewrite the sentences after replacing the underlined parts with words from the story. You may have to make some changes.

1. Virat made a heartfelt request to all his classmates to donate toys for the orphanage.
2. The thief walked with raised heels out of the house without making a sound.
3. The knight struck down the vicious dragon with a deadly blow.
4. You pamper your brother too much, giving in to his demands so easily.
5. He searched for his lost puppy with little hope left in his heart.
6. Pritha did not sleep well last night as she was having unpleasant dreams.
7. The match was to begin and the boxers stood facing each other in the ring.

verbs indicating expressions

Read this sentence.

'You think you are wiser than the newspaper?' Father **sneered**.

Here the verb *sneered* refers to Swami's father's facial expression, which suggests that he did not care much for Swami's opinions. We often use such verbs which refer to facial expressions.

B. Match the verbs/verb phrases indicating facial expressions, with their meanings.

Verbs/verb phrases	Meanings
1. grin	a. press lips together when one is angry or in deep thought
2. pout	b. smile broadly from ear to ear
3. frown	c. stare angrily
4. roll one's eyes	d. twist one's face in an expression of anger
5. scowl	e. to have a big happy smile on your face
6. purse one's lips	f. bring eyebrows together while thinking or in annoyance
7. glower	g. move eyes in a circle or look up to show irritation or impatience
8. beam	h. stick out lips, to show one is annoyed or to look attractive

Now make sentences of your own with any four of these words.

Grammar

You know that pronouns are words that are used in place of nouns. Pronouns agree with the nouns they replace in number and gender. They are of several types.

Personal pronouns are used in place of the names of people and things. These are *I, we, you, he, she, it, they, me, us, him, her,* and *them.*

Example: Swaminathan felt cut off from humanity. **He** was pained and angry.

Reflexive pronouns are used when we want to refer back to the subject of the sentence. In some cases, they can act as the object of the sentence if the subject and the object are the same.

Example: Swaminathan threw **himself** on his bed.

Demonstrative pronouns point to specific people and things. These are *this, that, these* and *those.*

Example: **That** is the room where Swami caught the housebreaker.

Interrogative pronouns are used to ask questions. The five interrogative pronouns are *who, what, which, whom* and *whose.*

Example: **Whom** did Swami attack at night?

A. Fill in the blanks with the suitable pronouns.

herself   who   this   she   which   ourselves   those   that

1. ______________ is for you and ______________ is for Sita.
2. Sally bought a bouquet of flowers for ______________.
3. Riya sings so beautifully. ______________ takes lessons from a famous musician.
4. ______________ of these dresses looks better?
5. These fruits are ripe, while ______________ are a week old.
6. ______________ called me on my phone?
7. We found ______________ alone on the empty road, with not a soul in sight.

The most commonly used punctuation marks are the fullstop (.), the comma (,), the question mark (?) and the exclamation mark (!).

A **full stop** is used to show a long pause. We use it when we want to end a statement or a command.

A **comma** is used to show a very short pause.

A **question mark** is used at the end of an interrogative sentence.

An **exclamation mark** is used at the end of a sentence which shows strong feelings such as happiness, sadness and anger.

B. Rewrite these sentences with the correct punctuation marks. Remember to use capital letters, wherever necessary.

1. What a delicious dish
2. what was the result of the match
3. oh no I just lost track of time
4. let us go for a stroll
5. sherlock holmes lived in london
6. please pack my pink dress white hat sunglasses and blue slippers
7. you live in lucknow dont you
8. have you seen the brown suitcase anywhere

apostrophe to show possession

Read this sentence.

And what about poor Munisami**'s** father, who spat out blood because the devil slapped his cheek?

Here, the apostrophe s after *Munisami* shows the relation between Munisami and his father.

An apostrophe (') is used to show that someone or something belongs or relates to someone or something else.

For plural nouns that already end in s, we add only the apostrophe *(')*.

Example: Swami gained all the boy**s'** admiration.

We add an apostrophe s *('s)* to irregular plural nouns that do not end in s.

Example: Swami and his friends gathered at the children**'s** park.

C. Rewrite the sentences adding apostrophe (') or apostrophe *s* ('s) in the correct places.

1. My friends mother baked a cake for us.
2. There was a teachers meeting today.
3. Womens cricket is gaining popularity in India.
4. The rabbits burrows are located deep in the woods.
5. The bearded man is Jacks uncle.
6. The butchers knife is very sharp.
7. The teams performances were appreciated by everyone.

Study Skills

Spelling

ie and *ei* words

Look at these words.

die tried relieved

In most words with the letters *i* and *e*, *i* is usually placed before *e*.
But there are exceptions where we spell the words with *ei*.
Examples: ceiling leisure

Read the meanings and complete the words by adding *ei* or *ie*.

1. s_ _ze: take hold of
2. n_ _ghbour: a person living next door
3. f_ _ld: an area of land
4. for_ _gn: of another country
5. pr_ _st: someone who performs religious duties
6. rec_ _ve: get something
7. h_ _ght: measurement from head to toe
8. ach_ _ve: succeed in doing something

Listening

listening for information

Listen to a passage about a boy who saved many lives and then answer the following questions.

1. Who was the local hero?
2. Which railway line is being spoken of?
3. What was the boy doing and what did he notice?
4. What did he do to stop the train?

5. What was the driver's reaction?
6. What inspired the boy?
7. What did the chief public relations officer of the East Central Railways say about the boy?

Dictation

You will now listen to a short story about Tenali Raman and write it down. Each sentence will be repeated twice. Listen carefully and be careful not to make any spelling errors.

Speaking

interview

In the story, Swaminathan was considered a hero in Malgudi after he was believed to have caught the infamous burglar. Imagine that you are a reporter from a local TV channel, who has been sent to interview Swami about the incident. Discuss and enact in pairs the questions that you would like to ask Swami, and the replies he would give. You could talk about the following points:

- the events leading up to his catching the housebreaker
- how he caught him and whether he had planned his course of action
- his feelings after foiling the burglary and being hailed as a hero
- his future plans, and whether he wants to be a police officer or a detective

Useful words and phrases

hobbies, games, army responsible, idea, courage, stern, attack, lesson, happy, proud, afraid, names, pilot, police, aim

Writing

writing a story

A. In 'A Hero', Swami acts in a brave manner without really meaning to. Write a humorous story about a person who does something out of fear, but which turns out to be an act of bravery. Your story should have a logical plot, well-developed characters and an interesting ending.

writing a dialogue

B. Imagine that you are Swaminathan and it's the morning after your adventure. You want to tell your best friend, Mani, about your experience. Write suitable dialogues for Swami and Mani, as you describe your heroic deed.
You can start in this way:

Swami: Mani, guess what happened last night!

Mani: What happened, Swami? I heard the police came to your house.

Now I can...

Self-Assessment

- o read and enjoy a humorous story about a boy's unintended heroism.
- o use words in context, and verbs indicating expressions.
- o understand and use the different types of pronouns, and punctuation marks, including apostrophe to show possession.
- o spell words with *ie-* and *ei-* correctly.
- o interview someone, pen a story and write dialogues.

Read at Leisure

Totto-Chan: The Little Girl at the Window: This book by Tetsuko Kuroyanagi is an account of childhood recollections from the World War II era, of a Japanese school girl who joins an unusual school in Tokyo that combined learning with fun, freedom and love.

Gangsta Granny: This humorous book by David Walliams is about Ben, who hates staying with his seemingly boring grandmother who only feeds him cabbage. She is later found to be an international jewel thief.

Answers to Take Off:

A. 1 – d (Charlie Chaplin) 2 – c (Edward Lear) 3 – e (Laurel and Hardy)
4 – a (Mr Bean) 5 – b (The Simpsons)

B. 1. pop music
2. bhangra
3. folk music
4. qawwali
5. bhajan
6. rap

nonsense poetry

6 The Power of Music

Sukumar Ray

Reading

Do you like to sing? Do people appreciate your singing? Read a funny poem about a man whose singing had rather unusual effects on his listeners.

When summer comes, we hear the hums
of Bhisma Lochan Sharma.
You catch his **strain** on hill and plain from Delhi
down to Burma
He sings as though he's **staked** his life, he sings
as though he's **hell-bent**;
The people, dazed, **retire** amazed although they
know it's well-meant.
They're **trampled** in the panic **rout** or **languish**
pale and sickly,
And plead, 'My friend, we're near our end, oh
stop your singing quickly!'
The bullock-carts are overturned, and horses
line the roadside;
But Bhisma Lochan, unconcerned, goes
booming out his **broadside**.
The wretched **brutes resent** the blare the hour
they hear it sounded,

What is heard in summer?

strain: the sound of music being played or sung
staked: risked something important
hell-bent: determined to do something even though the results may be bad
retire: withdraw or leave
trampled: (here) got stepped on heavily
rout: a disorderly retreat
languish: to become weaker
broadside: an aggressive attack in spoken or written words
brutes: (here) animals
resent: to feel bitter or angry about something

They **whine** and stare with feet in air or wonder
quite **confounded**.
The fishes dived below the lake in **frantic** search
for silence,
The very trees **collapse** and shake – you hear the
crash a mile hence –
And in the sky the feathered fly turn turtle[1] while
they're **winging**,
Again we cry, 'We're going to die, oh won't you
stop your singing?'
But Bhisma's soared beyond our reach[2], howe'er
we plead and grumble;
The **welkin** weeps[3] to hear his screech,
and mighty mansions tumble.
But now there comes a **billy goat**, a most
sagacious fellow,
He downs his horns and charges straight, with
bellow answ'ring bellow.
The strains of song are tossed and whirled by
blast of brutal violence,
And Bhisma Lochan grants the world the golden
gift of silence.

Translated by Sukanta Chaudhuri

What happens to the feathered fly?

Common idioms and proverbs

1. **turn turtle:** This idiom means to turn over completely while flying or sailing.

Literary terms

2. This is a **pun**. As the song becomes louder, it goes beyond the listeners' levels of tolerance. Bhisma himself is beyond the 'reach' or control of his listeners, as he doesn't listen to their pleas to stop singing.
3. This is an example of **alliteration**, as the 'w' sound is repeated in consecutive words.

whine: make a long high unpleasant sound because of pain
confounded: confused
frantic: hurried
collapse: fall down very suddenly
winging: flying
welkin: the sky or heaven
billy goat: a male goat
sagacious: wise
bellow: an angry shout in a loud, deep voice

About the poet

Sukumar Ray (1887–1923) was a Bengali poet, author, playwright, and illustrator. He is best remembered for his nonsense literature, including *Abol Tabol*, a collection of poems and the novella *HaJaBaRaLa*. He also brought new printing technology to India. He was the father of the celebrated filmmaker, Satyajit Ray.

Understanding the poem

A. Complete the sentences with words and phrases from the poem.

1. Bhisma's strain can be heard from ______________________.
2. The people languish as they look ______________________.
3. The bullock-carts are ______________, and ______________ line the roadside.
4. The song makes the trees ______________________.
5. The welkin weeps and the ______________________ tumble.
6. The strains of song are ______________ by blast of brutal violence.

B. Answer the questions with reference to context.

1. *He sings as though he's staked his life, he sings as though he's hell-bent;*
   a. Who is being referred to as 'he'?
   b. When is 'his' song heard and where?
   c. What happens to people as a result of hearing his song? Do you think they are really going to die because of it?
2. *The wretched brutes resent the blare the hour they hear it sounded...*
   a. What is the 'blare' that is being referred to?
   b. Who are the 'wretched brutes' and what do they do on hearing the 'blare'?
   c. Name the other creatures in the poem who are also affected by the 'blare'.
3. *...And Bhisma Lochan grants the world the golden gift of silence.*
   a. Why is the silence being referred to as a 'golden gift'?
   b. What is the literary device used in these lines? Point out two other instances from the poem.
   c. How did Bhisma Lochan finally fall silent?

Life Skills and Values — humour, appreciating music

1. Was Bhisma Lochan Sharma a good or a bad singer? Give examples from the poem to support your answer.
2. *The Power of Music* is a nonsense poem. It describes several situations which are absurd or not possible in real life. Make a list of these situations.

Vocabulary

compound nouns

A **compound noun** is formed by combining two nouns to make a completely new word. The meaning of the new word is usually different from either of its parts.

The two nouns in the compound noun may be hyphenated, separated by a space or joined together.

Examples: bullock + cart = **bullock-cart**
billy + goat = **billy goat**

A. Match the words in the two columns to form compound nouns.

Column A	Column B
1. well	a. office
2. good	b. moon
3. note	c. being
4. post	d. night
5. full	e. sticks
6. chop	f. book

B. Fill in the blanks with the compound nouns you have just formed.

1. I prefer using ______________ while having noodles.
2. Tina always looks after her parents' ______________.
3. Before going to bed, I regularly wish my parents ______________.
4. My father asked me to take this letter to the ______________.
5. The Taj Mahal looks splendid when there is a ______________.
6. The student wrote the questions down in his ______________.

homonyms

Read these sentences.

And in the sky the feathered **fly** turn turtle while they're winging... (fly = small flying insect with two wings)

Sunny saw the geese **fly** across the sky in a 'V' formation. (fly = move through air)

The word *fly* is a homonym.

Words which have the same spelling or pronunciation but different meanings are called **homonyms**.

C. Make two sentences with each of these homonyms. Use the word in a different sense for each sentence.

1. shake 2. plain 3. match 4. well 5. park 6. bright 7. kind

Activity

recitation

A. Listen to your teacher read the poem aloud. Then take turns and recite it in class. Remember to pause at the right places, and bring in elements of drama, by changing the pitch of your voice. As this is a humorous poem with a lot of action, you can also recite it in a comical, sing-song style.

completing a fact sheet

B. Work in pairs and collect information about a famous musician. You may work on Pandit Ravi Shankar, or Ustad Allah Rakha, both of whom you came across in the chapter, *The Concert*, in *Enriching English 5*. Then complete the given fact sheet.

1. Name of the musician: ____________________
2. His/her chosen field of music: ____________________
3. Nationality: ____________________
4. A teacher or person who inspired him/her: ____________________
5. His/her style: ____________________
6. Instrument he/she plays (if any): ____________________
7. Awards received by him/her: ____________________

Now I can... Self-Assessment

- read and enjoy a humorous poem about a singer's terrible songs.
- form compound nouns and use homonyms.
- recite a poem with the correct intonation and expressions.
- complete a fact sheet on a famous musician.

Read at Leisure

The Owl and the Pussy Cat: This nonsense poem by Edward Lear is about an owl and a pussy cat who set out to sea and decide to get married.

Stew Much: This nonsense poem by Sukumar Ray describes what happens when various animals, such as the duck and the porcupine, combine to form strange new species.

Project 1

A. In the chapter *Children of India*, you read about the various challenges children in India face while going to school.
With the help of your teacher, arrange a class visit to another school nearby. Observe the facilities provided there and interact with the students. Then, in groups of four, discuss the following points about the school visit and present it to your class.

- how their classrooms are different from yours
- how their playground is different from yours
- the teacher-student ratio
- some facilities which you found similar to your school's
- something you noticed in the school which you wished you had in your school
- something you would like to change in the school you visited

B. In the chapter *How I Taught My Grandmother to Read*, you read about the determination of the grandmother who decides to learn to read and write.
Now, design a brochure for a campaign in your school, titled 'Each One Teach One'.

'Each One Teach One' is a concept that tells us to help people who do not have access to education by teaching them how to read. The campaign's objective is to encourage students to take out some time to teach.

You can include the following elements in your brochure:

- First fold: a slogan and an image related to the theme 'Each One Teach One'
- Second fold: importance of knowing how to read and write. You can write about:
  a. why reading and writing is useful
  b. why we should promote the importance of knowing how to read and write
- Third fold: list the various ways one can implement 'Each One Teach One' like
  a. teaching your older relatives who could not receive education
  b. teaching your domestic help or their children to read and write
  c. teaching at any local orphanages

Making a Brochure

- Take an A4 sheet of paper.
- Turn the paper sideways so that the longer side is on the top.
- Use a pencil and a ruler to divide the page into three parts.
- Fold the left side towards the centre.
- Repeat the above step with the right side.
- The trifold paper that you get is your brochure!
  Use each side of the folds as a panel to write on.

IV

Health and Hygiene

Take Off

A. From the given list of words, choose those that you think are associated with the medical profession and fill in the boxes.

allergy	elementary	diagnosis	loyal	epidemic
cheeseburger	antibiotic	honesty	vaccination	nutrition

B. Look at the picture clues and fill in the boxes to show the things one should do to stay healthy.

short story

7 A Day's Wait

Ernest Hemingway

Reading

Good health is a gift that we truly value only when we fall quite sick. Read the story to understand a child's reaction to his sudden illness.

He came into the room to shut the windows while we were still in bed and I saw he looked ill. He was shivering, his face was white, and he walked slowly as though it ached to move.

'What's the matter, Schatz?'

'I've got a headache.'

'You better go back to bed.'

'No, I'm all right.'

'You go to bed. I'll see you when I'm dressed.'

But when I came downstairs, he was dressed, sitting by the fire, looking a very sick and miserable boy of nine years. When I put my hand on his forehead I knew he had a fever.

'You go up to bed,' I said, 'you're sick.'

'I'm all right,' he said.

When the doctor came, he took the boy's temperature.

'What is it?' I asked him.

'One hundred and two.'

Downstairs, the doctor left three different medicines in different coloured capsules with instructions for giving them. One was to bring down the fever, another a **purgative**, the third to overcome an acid condition. The germs of **influenza** can only exist in an acid condition, he explained.

purgative: a medicine that causes one to get rid of unwanted waste from the body

influenza: infection that leads to fever, aches and weakness

He seemed to know all about influenza and said there was nothing to worry about if the fever did not go above one hundred and four degrees. This was a light epidemic of flu and there was no danger if you avoided **pneumonia**.

Back in the room I wrote the boy's temperature down and made a note of the time to give the various capsules.

'Do you want me to read to you?'

'All right. If you want to,' said the boy. His face was very white and there were dark areas under his eyes. He lay still in bed and seemed very **detached** from what was going on. I read aloud from *Howard Pyle's Book of Pirates*; but I could see he was not following what I was reading.

Food for thought

Howard Pyle's Book of Pirates is a popular collection of adventure stories about pirates, written and illustrated by the American author Howard Pyle.

'How do you feel, Schatz?' I asked him.

'Just the same, so far,' he said.

I sat at the foot of the bed and read to myself while I waited for it to be time to give another capsule. It would have been natural for him to go to sleep, but when I looked up he was looking at the foot of the bed, staring very strangely.

'Why don't you try to go to sleep? I'll wake you up for the medicine.'

'I'd rather stay awake.'

After a while he said to me, 'You don't have to stay here with me, Papa, if it bothers you.'

'It doesn't bother me.'

'No, I mean you don't have to stay if it's going to bother you.'

I thought perhaps he was a little **light-headed** and after giving him the prescribed capsule at eleven o'clock, I went out for a while.

When did the narrator give Schatz the prescribed capsule?

It was a bright, cold day, the ground covered with a **sleet** that had frozen so that it seemed as if all the bare trees, the bushes, the cut **brush** and all the grass and the bare ground had been **varnished** with ice[1]. I took the young **Irish setter** for a little walk up the road and along a frozen **creek**, but it was difficult to stand or walk on the glassy surface and the red dog slipped and slithered and fell twice, hard.

Literary term

1. This is an example of **imagery**. The author uses these words to create a vivid picture of a landscape so frozen in ice that it appears polished and shiny.

---

pneumonia: a serious illness affecting one or both lungs that makes breathing difficult

detached: showing a lack of feeling

light-headed: feeling giddy or dizzy

sleet: a mixture of rain and snow

brush: small bushes and trees in a rough open area

varnished: polished so that the surface is hard, shiny and transparent

Irish setter: a breed of dogs found in Ireland, having a flat soft brownish-red coat

creek: a small river or stream

When we went back to the house, they said the boy had refused to let anyone come into the room.

'You can't come in,' he said. 'You mustn't get what I have.'

I went up to him and found him in exactly the position I had left him, white-faced, but with the tops of his cheeks **flushed** by the fever, staring still, as he had stared, at the foot of the bed. I took his temperature.

'What is it?'

'Something like a hundred,' I said. It was one hundred and two and four tenth.

'It was a hundred and two,' he said.

What was Schatz's exact temperature?

'Who said so?'

'The doctor.'

'Your temperature is all right,' I said. 'It's nothing to worry about.'

'I don't worry,' he said, 'but I can't keep from thinking.'

'Don't think,' I said. 'Just take it easy[2].'

'I'm taking it easy,' he said and looked straight ahead. He was **evidently** holding tight onto himself about something.

Common idioms and proverbs

2. **take it easy:** This idiom is used to tell somebody not to be worried or angry.

'Take this with water.'

'Do you think it will do any good?'

'Of course it will.'

I sat down and opened the *Pirate* book and **commenced** to read, but I could see he was not following, so I stopped.

'About what time do you think I'm going to die?' he asked.

'What?'

'About how long will it be before I die?'

'You aren't going to die. What's the matter with you?'

'Oh, yes, I am. I heard him say a hundred and two.'

'People don't die with a fever of one hundred and two. That's a silly way to talk.'

'I know they do. At school in France the boys told me you can't live with forty-four degrees. I've got a hundred and two.'

He had been waiting to die all day, ever since nine o'clock in the morning.

Food for thought

The Centigrade and Fahrenheit scales both measure temperature. The normal temperature for human beings is 36.9 degrees Centigrade. On the Fahrenheit scale, it is 98.4 degrees. A temperature above this is an indication of fever.

flushed: with a red face
evidently: clearly, obviously
commenced: began

'You poor Schatz,' I said. 'Poor old Schatz. It's like miles and kilometres. You aren't going to die. That's a different thermometer. On that thermometer, thirty-seven is normal. On this kind it's ninety-eight.'

'Are you sure?'

'Absolutely,' I said. 'It's like miles and kilometres. You know, like how many kilometres we make when we do seventy in the car?'

'Oh,' he said. But his gaze at the foot of his bed relaxed slowly. The hold over himself relaxed too, finally, and the next day it was very **slack** and he cried very easily at little things that were of no importance.

slack: loose

About the author

Ernest Hemingway (1899–1961) was an American author and journalist who won the Nobel Prize in Literature in 1954. He worked as an ambulance driver in World War I and as a reporter during World War II. His most famous works are *The Old Man and the Sea*, *For Whom the Bell Tolls* and *A Farewell to Arms*.

Comprehension

A. Write whether the following statements are true (T) or false (F). Correct the false statements.

1. Schatz said he had a stomach ache. ☐
2. The doctor said that influenza germs exist in an acid condition. ☐
3. It was a bright, cold day with the ground covered with sleet. ☐
4. The narrator's dog was an Irish setter. ☐
5. The narrator found Schatz staring out of the window. ☐
6. At the German school, Schatz had heard that one cannot live with a temperature of forty-four degrees. ☐

B. Answer the questions with reference to context.

1. *He seemed to know all about influenza and said there was nothing to worry about if the fever did not go above one hundred and four degrees.*
   a. Who is 'he' here? Whose fever is being talked about?
   b. Why did 'he' say that there was nothing to worry about?
   c. What medicines did 'he' prescribe?

2. *'You poor Schatz,' I said. 'Poor old Schatz. It's like miles and kilometres.'*
   a. Who said this and to whom? Why was the person spoken to called 'poor'?
   b. What was 'like miles and kilometres'?
   c. What were the normal temperature readings?

3. *The hold over himself relaxed too, finally, and the next day it was very slack and he cried very easily at little things that were of no importance.*
   a. Who is 'he' here?
   b. What is meant by relaxing 'the hold over himself'? Why could 'he' then cry easily over unimportant things?
   c. Do you think 'he' had a valid reason to behave this way?

Life Skills and Values — importance of clear understanding

1. Why do you think Schatz did not tell the narrator that he expected to die till the end? What does it say about his character?
2. Do you think it is important to ask questions when in doubt? Explain with examples from the text.
3. 'Weak and fearful thoughts weaken the spirit/body and cheerful thoughts strengthen the spirit/body.' Explain how this is true for Schatz in the given passage.

Vocabulary

words related to health

Read the clues and solve the crossword. You can take the help of a dictionary.

Across

2. a thick sweet medicinal liquid
6. instructions given by the doctor for medicines
8. the amount of medicine to be given
9. a person trained to take care of sick people
10. the act of surgery

Down

1. a disease that spreads rapidly
3. a place where sick and injured people are treated
4. an instrument for measuring temperature
5. a strip of cloth used to bind a wound
7. an illness caused by bacteria or a virus

Grammar

direct and indirect speech

Read these sentences.
Schatz said, 'I have got a headache.'
Schatz said that he had got a headache.

The first sentence is in **direct speech** as the exact words of the speaker are quoted.

The second sentence is in **indirect speech** as the words of the speaker are reported, and not directly quoted.

In indirect speech, we do not use inverted commas, but make use of reporting words such as *said, asked, exclaimed* and *requested*.

Look at this chart for the changes we make while converting direct speech to indirect speech.

Direct speech ⟶ Indirect speech

- **person**: the first person *(I, we)* ⟶ the third person *(he, she, they)*
- **pronoun**: *this* ⟶ *that*; *these* ⟶ *those*
- **time/place words**: *now* ⟶ *then*; *today* ⟶ *that day*; *tomorrow* ⟶ *the next day/the following day*; *here* ⟶ *there*
- **tense**: present tense ⟶ past tense; past tense ⟶ past perfect tense

A. Rewrite these sentences in indirect speech.

1. Mridula asked her mother, 'May I have some ice cream?'
2. 'Stop what you are doing right now,' the policeman shouted.
3. Ritu said to Rohini, 'Let's study at my house tomorrow.'
4. I said to my brother, 'You need to start exercising regularly.'
5. The teacher asked the students, 'Isn't it lunch break yet?'
6. Sana asked her friend, 'Shall we go to the library today?'
7. He said, 'Joanna, come here for a minute.'
8. Mother said, 'Rohan, pick up your crayons from the floor.'

subject-verb agreement

For a sentence to be grammatically correct, the main verb should agree with the subject in person and number. This is called the **agreement of the subject and verb.**

Look at some of the rules of subject-verb agreement.

- When the subject is singular, the verb should be singular. When the subject is plural, the verb is also plural.
  Example: His <u>face</u> **was** very white and there **were** dark <u>areas</u> under his eyes.
- Two or more subjects joined by *and* take a plural verb.
  Example: The bare trees, the bushes, and all the grass **were** covered with frost.
- If a subject comes after *each* or *every*, the verb is usually singular. The same rule applies to pronouns like *anyone*, *anybody*, *no one*, *nobody*, *someone*, and *somebody*.
  Examples: Every boy in the school **gave** Schatz the wrong information.
  Nobody **should believe** in wrong information.
- When the subject is made up of two or more nouns joined by correlative conjunctions like *either...or, neither...nor*, the verb agrees with the noun or pronoun that is placed closest to it.
  Examples: Either the doctor or his assistants **are arriving** tomorrow.
  Neither the nurses nor the doctor **is arriving** tomorrow.

B. Fill in the blanks with the correct words.

1. Bread, butter and eggs _______________ (is/are) common breakfast items.
2. Each of the soldiers _______________ (has/have) shown tremendous bravery.
3. That pair of trousers _______________ (is/are) in the cupboard.
4. Somebody _______________ (is/are) coming to repair the fridge.
5. The cow, along with the horses, _______________ (was/were) grazing on the field.
6. Neither Rehaan nor Urja _______________ (has/have) arrived yet.
7. No one in the playground _______________ (is/are) too noisy.
8. The trials for the games _______________ (was/were) very tiring.

Study Skills

Pronunciation

stressed and unstressed syllables

In words which have two syllables, the syllable that is said with emphasis is the **stressed syllable**. The **unstressed syllable** is that part of the word which has no emphasis.

Say these words aloud.

birthday perhaps → per**haps**

Notice that the syllables in bold are said with more stress. So, *birth* and *haps* are the stressed syllables, whereas *day* and *per* are the unstressed syllables in these words.

Say these words aloud. Then, divide them into syllables and identify the stressed and unstressed syllables.

1. sandwich
2. exhaust
3. purple
4. disturb
5. teacher
6. reduce
7. mistake
8. selfish
9. basin

Listening

listening for details

Listen to a dialogue between a mother and her son and then answer the following questions.

1. What did Rahul's mother ask him to wear?
2. Which two reasons did Rahul give for not requiring gloves?
3. What did his mother wish he would do?
4. What did Rahul have the following week?
5. What did Rahul's mother finally say to make him obey? What was his reply?

Speaking

making and responding to suggestions

Imagine that everyone around you has been falling ill due to change of seasons. Work in pairs and have a conversation about the probable reasons and the ways in which we should try to remain fit.

You can talk about these points.

- the importance of taking precautions
- health should not be taken for granted
- the effects of change of seasons
- good habits to follow (avoid junk food, not get wet in rain, sleep on time...)

Useful words and phrases

Making suggestions	Responding to suggestions
• I think/I feel...	• Yes, you are right...
• Why don't you...	• That's a good idea...
• You should/might...	• I should be...
• You may/do...	• Thank you, that would help...

Writing

Look at the given picture and then write a paragraph based on the scene. You may use the following points.

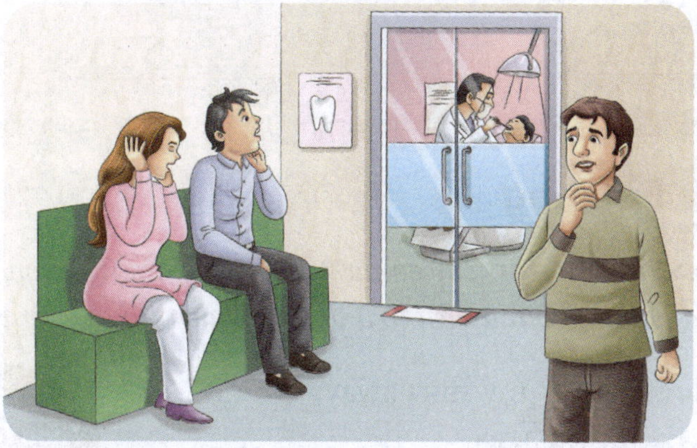

- the dental procedure
- the patient's feelings
- the dentist's opinions and instructions
- the outcome of the procedure
- the reactions of waiting patients

Now I can...

Self-Assessment

- o read and understand a story about a sick boy and his misgivings.
- o identify words related to health.
- o use direct and indirect speech and follow the rules of subject-verb agreement.
- o pronounce stressed and unstressed syllables.
- o make and respond to suggestions, and write a picture composition.

Read at Leisure

What Katy Did: This book by Susan Coolidge is about a mischievous young girl Katy who must draw on courage and good humour to see her through an accident that leaves her bedridden.

Kid Docs: This book by Jennie Lynne tells the story of child prodigies who were selected at just three years old to undergo intensive medical training as part of an experiment called *Kid Docs*.

8 The Doctor

Sir Alan Patrick Herbert

Reading

Do you think doctors can sometimes scare patients even though they have our best interests at heart? Read a poem about a visit to a doctor which takes a strange turn.

The doctor took my shirt away;
He did it for the best;
He said, 'It's very cold today,'
And took away my **vest**;
Then, having nothing more to say,
He hit me in the chest.
Oh, he did **clout** my ribs about
Till I was bruised and red,
Then stood and listened to my spine
To see if I was dead,
And when I shouted 'Ninety-nine!'
He simply shook his head.
He made me hop about the hall[1],
And **savagely** he said,
'There's nothing wrong with you at all.
You'd better go to bed!

'Oh you must eat no scrap of meat,
No rabbit, bird, or fish;
Apart from that have what you please,
But no potato, bread, or cheese...

Food for thought

Doctors tap patients' ribs to listen to the sounds and check the condition of the organs inside the chest cavity, based on how dull or clear the sounds are.

They also make patients call out numbers like *sixty six* and *ninety-nine*, and listen to the sounds in their chest cavity, to check lung health. In healthy lungs, the sounds are faint and muffled. Unhealthy lungs produce clearer sounds.

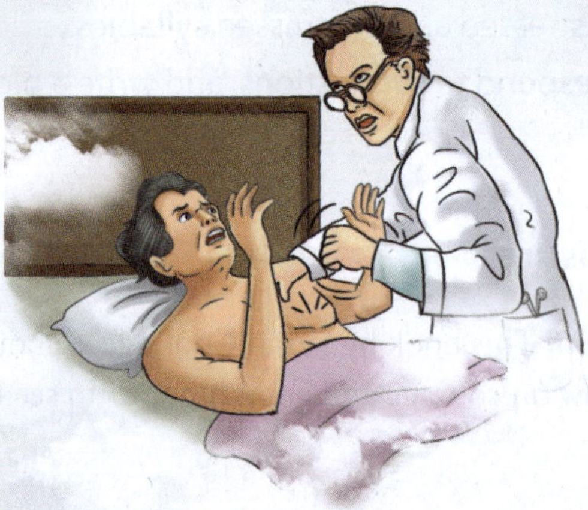

vest: an undergarment covering the body from the shoulders to the hips, made of cotton or nylon

clout: hit somebody hard, especially with your hand

savagely: roughly

Common idioms and proverbs

a clean bill of health: This idiom refers to a report that says somebody is healthy or that something is in good condition.

Example: Doctors gave him *a clean bill of health* after a series of tests.

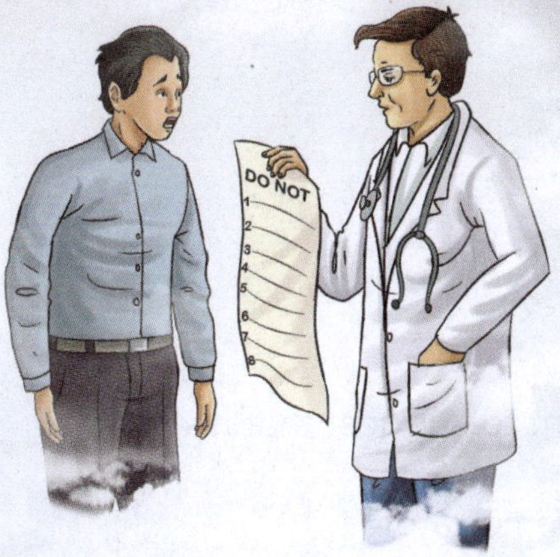

... Have any other foods but these
Have anything you wish[2]!

'You must not hum, or read a book,
You must not eat or drink;
You must not bicycle or run,
You must not talk to anyone;
It's better not to think.
A daily bath I don't advise;
It's dangerous to snore;
But let your life be otherwise
As active as before.
And don't imagine you are ill,
I beg you not to **mope**;
There's nothing wrong with you — but still,
While there is life, there's hope.'

I woke and screamed a **hideous** scream
As greedy children do
Who eat too much vanilla cream
For I was having the 'flu;
And it was just an awful dream
But all the same, it's true.

(abridged)

Which activity is dangerous, according to the doctor?

Literary terms

1. This is an example of **alliteration**, where the 'h' sound is repeated in words placed close together.
2. This is an example of **irony**, where although the doctor allows the narrator to eat anything he wishes, he means the exact opposite by banning various food items from the narrator's diet.

mope: feel gloomy or sad
hideous: terrifying, very ugly or unpleasant

About the poet

Sir Alan Patrick Herbert (1890–1971) was a British playwright, author and a Member of Parliament. He often presented serious ideas in a humorous and witty way. He wrote novels like *The Secret Battle*, *The House by the River*, as well as plays like *Tantivy Towers* and *Bless the Bride*.

Understanding the poem

A. Choose the correct answer.

1. The doctor took away the narrator's shirt and ______________ (tie/vest/shoes).
2. He told the narrator to go to ______________ (school/jail/bed).
3. The narrator should not eat a scrap of ______________ (meat/cake/bread).
4. He advised the narrator to not take a ______________ (jog/swim/bath).
5. The narrator actually had ______________ (chicken pox/flu/malaria).

B. Answer the questions with reference to context.

1. *Oh, he did clout my ribs about*
   Till I was bruised and red...
   a. Who is being referred to as 'he' in these lines?
   b. What were the things he did next?
   c. Note down the lines in the stanza which seem to suggest that his actions were cruel.
   d. What was 'his' conclusion after examining the narrator?
2. *Have any other foods but these*
   Have anything you wish!
   a. What were the food items the narrator was asked to avoid?
   b. Do you think the narrator could indeed have anything he wished?
   c. Mention any three things that he was asked not to do, immediately afterwards.
3. *And it was just an awful dream*
   But all the same, it's true.
   a. How did the narrator wake up from the dream?
   b. Whom does he compare himself to in this stanza?
   c. Why do you think the narrator says that the dream is true?

Life Skills and Values

humour

1. The poem describes in an exaggerated way the things which doctors often do. Note down the things mentioned in the poem which a doctor is unlikely to say or do in real life.
2. The narrator portrays the doctor as a scary figure. Do you agree?
3. Did you find the poem humorous? Answer with examples from the poem.

Vocabulary

rhyme scheme

Look at this stanza from the poem.

The doctor took my shirt away;	(a)
He did it for the best;	(b)
He said, 'It's very cold today,'	(a)
And took away my vest;	(b)
Then, having nothing more to say,	(a)
He hit me in the chest.	(b)

In the stanza, the first, third and fifth lines rhyme with each other. The second, fourth and sixth lines also rhyme. This rhyming pattern, indicated by the letters *a* and *b*, is called the **rhyme scheme** of the poem. Here, it is *ababab*.

A. Identify the rhyme schemes of these verses.

1. 'A daily bath I don't advise; [a]
   It's dangerous to snore; [b]
   But let your life be otherwise [ ]
   As active as before. [ ]
   And don't imagine you are ill, [ ]
   I beg you not to mope; [ ]
   There's nothing wrong with you — but still, [ ]
   While there is life, there's hope.' [ ]

2. There was an Old Person of Dover, [ ]
   Who rushed through a field of blue Clover; [ ]
   But some very large bees, [ ]
   Stung his nose and his knees, [ ]
   So he very soon went back to Dover. [ ]

Activity

poster making

India has had several outbreaks of swine flu in the past few years. Make a poster to raise awareness about the disease, including the precautionary measures to be taken in case of an outbreak. Give a suitable title to your poster and include these points.

- how the disease spreads
- symptoms and treatment
- precautionary measures
- emergency helplines

Now I can... Self-Assessment

- o read and enjoy a funny poem about a strange encounter with a doctor.
- o identify the rhyme schemes of poems.
- o make a poster.

Read at Leisure

The Dentist and the Crocodile: This humorous poem by Roald Dahl is about a dentist who is terrified when a crocodile visits his office, asking to have his teeth 'repaired'.

Cleanliness: In this poem by Charles Lamb, a child is scolded for not washing his hands and is then explained the benefits of maintaining good hygiene.

V

Encounters with the Wild

Take Off

A. With the help of the clues given in the box, complete the sentences and discover interesting facts about scorpions.

night	glow	ten years	underwater	ride	courtship	2000

1. Baby scorpions ______________ on their mother's back till their shells become hard.
2. A wild scorpion lives up to ______________.
3. Scorpions usually have a long ______________ dance.
4. Scorpions ______________ under ultraviolet light.
5. There are around ______________ scorpion species.
6. Scorpions usually hunt at ______________.
7. Scorpions can live ______________ for about 48 hours.

B. Do you know what these endangered animals are hunted for? Work in pairs and answer.

1. Amur leopard

4. Hawksbill sea turtle

horns	fur
shells	meat
skin	tusks

2. African rhinoceros

5. Cross River gorilla

3. Sumatran elephant

6. Chinese alligator

adventure

9 An Unexpected Guest

Gerald Durrell

Reading

Have you ever looked at a garden wall and found a whole different world there? Read this story of a young boy and his escapades with the inhabitants of such a wall.

The crumbling wall that surrounded the sunken garden alongside the house was a rich hunting ground for me.

The shyest of the wall creatures were the most dangerous; you hardly ever saw one unless you looked for it, and yet there must have been several hundred living in the cracks of the wall. Slide a knife-blade carefully under a piece of the loose plaster and **lever** it gently away from the brick, and there, **crouching** beneath it, would be a little black scorpion an inch long, looking as though he were made out of polished chocolate.

Who were the shyest of the wall creatures?

They were weird-looking things, with their flattened, oval bodies, their neat, crooked legs, the enormous crab-like claws, **bulbous** and neatly jointed as **armour**, and the tail like a string of brown beads ending in a **sting** like a rose thorn. The scorpion would lie there quietly as you examined him, only raising his tail in an almost apologetic gesture of warning if you breathed too hard on him. If you kept him in the sun too long, he would simply turn his back on you and walk away under another section of plaster.

I grew very fond of these scorpions. I found them to be pleasant, **unassuming** creatures with the most charming habits. Provided you did nothing silly or clumsy (like putting your hand on one), they treated you with respect, their one desire being to get away and hide as quickly as possible.

By crouching under the wall at night with a torch, I managed to catch some brief glimpses of their wonderful **courtship** dances. They stood and **waltzed** slowly in circles among the moss cushions, claw in claw.

---

lever: move something in a particular direction, by using a lot of effort

crouching: keeping body close to ground by bending legs

bulbous: shaped liked a bulb, round and fat in an ugly way

armour: special metal clothing that soldiers wore in the past to protect their bodies while fighting

sting: the sharp pointed part of an insect or creature that can pierce the skin, leaving a painful and poisonous wound

unassuming: not wanting to draw attention to themselves

courtship: the special way animals behave to attract mates

waltzed: danced

The family had forbidden scorpions in the house, despite my arguments in favour of them. Then one day I found a fat female scorpion in the wall, wearing what at first glance appeared to be a pale **fawn** fur coat. Closer inspection showed that this strange garment was made up of a mass of tiny babies clinging to the mother's back. I was delighted by this family, and made up my mind to smuggle them to my bedroom so that I might keep them and watch them grow up. With great care, I placed the mother and her family into a matchbox, and hurried to the villa.

It was rather unfortunate that just as I entered the door, lunch should be served. I placed the matchbox carefully on the **mantelpiece** in the drawing room, so that the scorpions could get plenty of air, and made my way to the dining room and joined the family for the meal. **Dawdling** over my food, quietly feeding Roger under the table and listening to the family arguing, I completely forgot about my exciting new **captures**. At one point, Larry, having finished eating, walked to the mantelpiece and picked up the matchbox. Without any idea of my **impending doom** I watched him interestedly as, still talking, he opened the matchbox.

What had the family forbidden?

Now, I maintain to this day that the female scorpion meant no harm. She was nervous and a **trifle** annoyed at being shut up in a matchbox for so long, and so she took the first opportunity to escape. She **hoisted** herself out of the box with great rapidity, her babies clinging on desperately, and **scuttled** on to the back of Larry's hand. There, not quite certain what to do next, she paused, her sting curved up at the ready. Larry, feeling the movement of her claws, glanced down to see what it was, and from that moment on, things got very confusing.

He uttered a roar of fright that made Lugaretzia drop a plate and brought Roger out from beneath the table, barking wildly. With a **flick** of his hand, he sent the unfortunate scorpion flying down the table. She landed midway between Margo and Leslie, scattering babies like **confetti** as she thumped on the cloth. Thoroughly enraged at this treatment, the creature **sped** towards Leslie, her sting quivering with anger. Leslie leapt to his feet, overturning his chair, and flicked out desperately with his napkin, sending the scorpion rolling across the cloth towards Margo, who let out a scream that any railway engine would have been proud to produce. Mother, bewildered by this sudden change from peace to utter confusion, put on her glasses and peered down the table to see what was the cause.

At that moment, Margo, in a vain attempt to stop the scorpion, hurled a glass of water at it.

What was Margo's scream compared with?

fawn: light yellow-brown colour
mantelpiece: a shelf above a fireplace
dawdling: taking a long time
captures: (here) things taken or seized
impending: going to happen
doom: a terrible event one cannot avoid
trifle: slightly
hoisted: raised
scuttled: ran with quick short steps
flick: sudden quick movement
confetti: small pieces of coloured paper that people throw
sped: moved along quickly

The shower missed the animal completely, but successfully **drenched** Mother, who, not being able to stand cold water, lost her breath and sat gasping at the end of the table, unable even to **protest**.

The scorpion had now gone to ground[1] under Leslie's plate, while her babies **swarmed** wildly all over the table. Roger, also puzzled by the panic, but determined to do his share, ran round and round the room, barking wildly.

'Look out! Look out! They're coming!' screamed Margo.

'All we need is a book,' roared Leslie; 'don't panic, hit 'em with a book.'

'What on earth's the *matter* with you all?' Mother kept **imploring**, **mopping** her glasses.

'It's that boy... he'll kill the lot of us ... Look at the table... knee-deep in scorpions...'

'Stop **screeching** and get a book, for God's sake... *Shut up*, Roger... '

'By the grace of God I wasn't bitten...'

'Look out... there's another one... Quick, quick...'

'But *how* did the scorpions get on the table, dear?'

'That boy... Every matchbox in the house is a death trap[2]...'

'Look out, it's coming towards me... Quick, quick, do something...'

'Hit it with your knife ... *your knife*... Go on, hit it...'

Since no one had bothered to explain things to him, Roger was under the mistaken impression that the family was being attacked, and that it was his duty to defend them.

Common idioms and proverbs

1. **go to ground:** This idiom means to hide, especially to escape somebody who is chasing them.

Literary term

2. This is a **metaphor**. Every matchbox is being compared to a death trap since the scorpion came out of one, and could have stung someone.

---

drenched: soaked
protest: to disagree or show objection
swarmed: moved together
imploring: asking anxiously
mopping: wiping
screeching: making a loud high unpleasant sound

As Lugaretzia was the only stranger in the room, he came to the conclusion that she must be the responsible party, so he bit her in the ankle. This did not help matters much.

By the time order returned, all the baby scorpions had hidden themselves under various plates and bits of cutlery. Eventually, after many pleas on my part, backed up by Mother, Leslie's suggestion that the whole lot be **slaughtered** was rejected. While the family, still shaking, went to the drawing room, I spent half an hour rounding up the babies, picking them up in a teaspoon, and returning them to their mother's back. Then I carried them outside on a saucer and, very unwillingly released them on the garden wall.

The results of this incident were many. Larry developed a **phobia** about matchboxes and opened them with great **caution**, a handkerchief wrapped around his hand. Lugaretzia limped around the house, her ankle covered in yards of bandage, for weeks after the bite had healed, and every morning, showed us how the **scabs** were doing.

But from my point of view, the worst fallout of the whole affair was that Mother decided I was running wild again, and that it was high time I received a little more education.

Why did Lugaretzia limp around the house?

slaughtered: be killed
phobia: strong unreasonable fear
caution: great care which one takes in order to avoid possible danger
scabs: hard dry coverings that form over wounds as they heal

About the author

Gerald Durrell (1925–1995) was a British naturalist, conservationist, author and zookeeper. Durrell's interest in animals grew after moving to Corfu in Greece with his family in 1935, and he started to collect local creatures as pets. Some of his famous works are *My Family and Other Animals* and *The Garden of Gods*, the latter based on his experiences in Corfu.

Comprehension

A. Fill in the blanks with the correct words.

1. The little black scorpion looked as if he was made out of polished __________ (steel/wood/chocolate).
2. The fat female scorpion seemed to be wearing a pale __________ (brown/fawn/yellow) fur coat.
3. The author was quietly feeding __________ (Roger/Larry/Margo) under the table.
4. Margo hurled a __________ (knife/table napkin/glass of water) at the scorpion.
5. The scorpion babies were picked up in a __________ (teaspoon/saucer/shoe).
6. After the incident, Larry developed a phobia about __________ (scorpions/matchboxes/mantelpieces).

B. Answer the questions.

1. What fascinated the author about scorpions? Describe their courtship dance, as viewed by the author.
2. What did the author smuggle inside a matchbox and why?
3. Why was the female scorpion agitated? What did she do after Larry opened the matchbox?
4. Describe the scene caused by Larry, Leslie and Margo at the lunch table.
5. Why did the author's mother sit gasping at the end of the table?
6. How did Roger try to defend the family?
7. What was the worst fallout of the whole affair according to the author?

C. Answer the questions with reference to context.

1. *'Look out! Look out! They are coming!'*
   a. Who said these words? Who were coming?
   b. What were the two things mentioned as weapons to hit 'them'?
   c. Why couldn't the author's mother understand the cause of the commotion?

Life Skills and Values — appreciation for wildlife

1. Do you think the author should have picked up the scorpion from the wall? Why?
2. The author's pleas to let the scorpions live were supported by his mother. What does this tell you about her character?

Vocabulary

animal idioms

A. Match these animal idioms with their meanings. You may take the help of a dictionary.

Idioms	Meanings
1. hold your horses	a. annoy somebody very much
2. let the cat out of the bag	b. feeling uncomfortable because of unfamiliar surroundings
3. the lion's share	c. to become used to something very easily
4. get somebody's goat	d. to tell a secret carelessly or by mistake
5. like a duck to water	e. careless or clumsy, especially in a situation where skill and care is needed
6. a bull in a china shop	f. don't take an action hurriedly without thinking about it first
7. a fish out of water	g. the largest or best part of something

B. Fill in the blanks with the idioms from the previous exercise. You may have to make some changes.

1. Rohit got ______________ of the pie, because he was grandmother's favourite.
2. Meera ______________ by telling Vani about her surprise birthday party.
3. Mainak is talking loudly even after I told him not to, trying to ______________.
4. Ria felt like ______________ at the pottery class for the first few days.
5. He did not listen to us and charged into the room like ______________.
6. Rohini took to her bike ______________, as if she was born to ride.
7. ______________! Let's not take this route without checking the map.

similes

Read this line.

She landed midway between Margo and Leslie, scattering babies **like confetti** as she thumped on the cloth.

Here the scattering of the scorpion's babies has been compared with confetti being thrown, in every direction. This is a **simile**.

C. Complete the similes with the given words.

log	midnight	rose	whistle	bat	snow	cucumber

1. The old lady who lives next door is as blind as a ______.
2. After clearing away a lot of clutter, my room is now as clean as a ______.
3. The kitten Sana brought home yesterday is as white as ______.
4. As she blushed, her cheeks turned red like a ______.
5. He remained as cool as a ______ and ultimately won the debate.
6. It was as dark as ______ inside the deep, lush forest.
7. After working the whole day, I was tired and slept like a ______.

Grammar

transitive and intransitive verbs

Read these sentences.

With great care, I **placed** the mother and her family into a matchbox.
The scorpion **landed** midway between Margo and Leslie.

In the first sentence, the verb *(placed)* needs an object, *(the mother and her family)* to make complete sense. The **object** of a verb is a noun or pronoun that receives the action of the verb. Such verbs are called transitive verbs.
In the second sentence, the verb *(landed)* completes the meaning of the sentence, without requiring an object.

A **transitive verb** is a verb which needs an object to complete its meaning.

An **intransitive verb** makes complete sense by itself. It does not need an object to complete its meaning.

Intransitive verbs can stand alone or may be followed by a phrase that gives information about the action.

A. Underline the verbs in these sentences and identify them as transitive (T) or intransitive (IT).

1. The river flowed down the hill. ☐
2. The roller coaster ride is thrilling. ☐
3. Geeta bought strawberries from the market. ☐
4. The cook made pasta for dinner. ☐

5. John swims very well. ☐
6. The school bus arrived on time. ☐
7. The envelope contained important letters. ☐
8. The dog is sleeping on the rug. ☐

types of adverbs and their positions

You know that an adverb is a word that is used to modify or add information to a verb, an adjective or another adverb.

Look at this table which explains the functions of the various types of adverbs.

Types	Places	Examples
Adverbs of manner tell us how the action takes place.	after the verb or after the direct object of the verb	Roger came out from beneath the table, barking **wildly**.
Adverbs of time tell us when the action takes place.	at the end of the sentence	I was crouching under the wall **at night**.
Adverbs of place tell us where the action takes place.	after the verb	The scorpions would lie **there**.
Adverbs of frequency tell us how often the action takes place.	between the subject of the sentence and the verb	You **hardly** ever saw one.
Adverbs of degree tell us how intensely the action takes place.	before the verb, adverb or adjective it modifies	If you breathe **too** hard on him, he might attack you.

B. Insert the adverbs in the correct places and identify their types.

1. She goes to the library. (rarely)
2. The airhostess spoke to the passengers. (calmly)
3. They missed their train. (nearly)
4. The nightingale sang. (sweetly)
5. They will announce the winners. (now)
6. My father leaves by 8 a.m. (always)
7. Salim was satisfied with his painting. (quite)
8. I met my cousin. (here)

Study Skills

Dictionary Skills

finding meanings of words

Read these words aloud, and look at the way they are pronounced. These words have multiple meanings. Use your dictionary and write the correct meaning of the word based on its pronunciation.

1. live (rhymes with *dive*)
2. bow (rhymes with *row*)
3. wind (rhymes with *kind*)
4. lead (rhyming with *seed*)
5. read (rhyming with *bed*)

Listening

listening for details

Listen to a poem about different animals and fill in the blanks.

1. The ______________ (cat/dog) will come when called.
2. The monkey's ______________ (neck/cheek) is very bald.
3. The ______________ (parrot/goat) does not know what she says.
4. The horse will draw a ______________ (cart/chaise).
5. The squirrel likes a ______________ (nut/fruit).
6. The ______________ (wolf's/buzzard's) eyes are shut.
7. The ______________ (lark/linnet) sings in the tree.
8. The swan is said to be ______________ (gentle/proud).

Speaking

expressing an opinion

In the story, you read about the author's wish to bring home and keep wild creatures as pets. But most animals would likely prefer to live free in their natural habitat. Do you feel that man and nature can co-exist peacefully? Express your opinion in the class. You may use instances from the story to support your ideas.

Useful words and phrases

Man

- predator/destroyer/ protector of nature
- love for animals
- desire to domesticate

Nature

- animals survive best in their habitat
- loss of habitat forces them to move into human territories, leading to capture and loss of lives

Writing

What do you think would have happened if the author's mother had allowed the scorpions to be killed, or, if some baby scorpions had remained in the house? Write an alternate ending to the story, imagining yourself to be the author.

Now I can... **Self-Assessment**

- o read and enjoy an adventurous story about an encounter with scorpions.
- o understand and use idioms and similes.
- o identify transitive and intransitive verbs, and different types of adverbs and note their positions.
- o express an opinion on a topic.
- o write an alternate ending to the story.

Read at Leisure

Black Beauty: This book by Anna Sewell is about a handsome, sweet-tempered horse with a strong spirit, whose life changes from one of comfort and kindness to hard labour and cruelty.

The Story of Doctor Dolittle: This book by Hugh Lofting is about the adventures of a doctor who is able to befriend animals, because he can speak in their language.

10 Hunting Snake

Judith Wright

Reading

What would you do if you ever came face-to-face with a snake? Read this poem about an encounter between two people and a snake.

Sun-warmed in this late season's **grace**
under the autumn's gentlest sky
we walked, and froze half-through a pace.
The great black snake went **reeling** by.

Head down, tongue **flickering** on the **trail**
he **quested** through the **parting** grass[1],
sun glazed his curves of diamond scale[2]
and we lost breath to see him pass.

What track he followed, what small food
fled living from his fierce **intent**,
we **scarcely** thought; still as we stood
our eyes went with him as he went.

Cold, dark and splendid he was gone
into the grass that hid his prey.
We took a deeper breath of day,
looked at each other, and went on.

What season is spoken of in the poem?

grace: kindness
reeling: moving in an unsteady way; swaying
flickering: moving with small quick movements
trail: a track, sign or smell that can be followed while hunting
quested: searched for something difficult to find
parting: moving away
intent: purpose, aim
scarcely: only just; almost not

Literary terms

1. This is an example of **personification**. The grass is imagined as parting themselves to make way for the snake.
2. This is a **metaphor**. The brilliance of the snake's sunlit scales is compared to dazzling diamonds.

About the poet

Judith Arundell Wright (1915–2000) was an Australian poet and the recipient of the Queen's Gold medal for poetry. An environmentalist, she campaigned for the preservation of local flora and fauna. Some of her well-known works are *The Two Fires, Birds, The Other Half and Magpies.*

Understanding the poem

A. Choose the correct answer.

1. The poet describes the weather as ______________.
   a. cold b. warm c. stormy
2. The ______________ snake went reeling by.
   a. great, brown b. gorgeous, black c. great, black
3. The snake went through the parting ______________.
   a. grass b. weeds c. reeds
4. The sun glazed the snake's curves of ______________ scale.
   a. ruby b. diamond c. emerald
5. Seeing the snake, the poet and her companion ______________.
   a. stood still b. screamed c. started running

B. Answer the questions with reference to context.

1. *...we walked, and froze half-through a pace.*
   a. Who are referred to as 'we' here?
   b. When and where were they walking?
   c. Why did they freeze?
2. *What track he followed, what small food*
   fled living from his fierce intent,
   we scarcely thought; still as we stood
   our eyes went with him as he went.
   a. Who is 'he'? Where did he go?
   b. What was his 'fierce intent'?
   c. Why did they stand still and not think at all?
   d. Point out the literary device used in the line 'we scarcely thought; still as we stood'.

3. *We took a deeper breath of day,*
looked at each other, and went on.
   a. Why did they take 'a deeper breath of day'? What do you understand by the expression?
   b. Why do you think they looked at each other?
   c. Do you think they were holding their breath all this while? If so, why?

Life Skills and Values — appreciating nature and wildlife

1. What do you think the poet means by the expression 'late season's grace'?
2. Why does the poet describe the snake as 'cold, dark and splendid'? Do you feel the poet admires the snake, but is afraid of him, at the same time? Explain your answer with lines from the poem.

Vocabulary

imagery

Read this line.
Sun-warmed in this late season's grace...
This line helps us to feel the warmth of the sun that the poet is experiencing. This is an instance of touch imagery.

Look at the diagram which shows the different kinds of imagery. Then explain the imagery in these lines from the poem.

1. under the autumn's gentlest sky
2. The great black snake went reeling by.
3. Head down, tongue flickering on the trail/he quested through the parting grass
4. sun glazed his curves of diamond scale
5. What track he followed, what small food/fled living from his fierce intent
6. Cold, dark and splendid he was gone

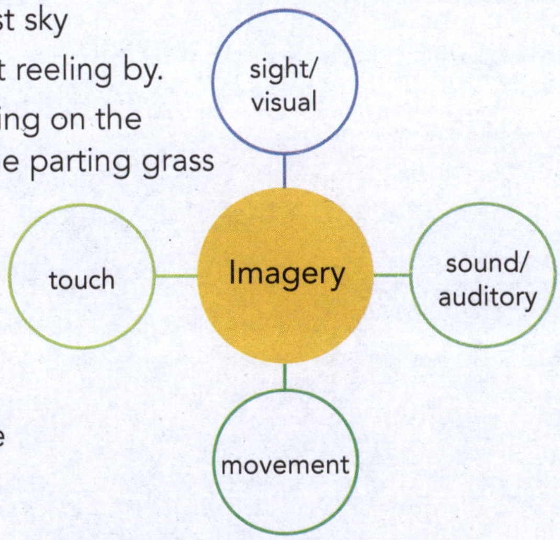

Activity

Indiscriminate hunting, poaching and loss of habitat has resulted in endangering many species all over the world. Make a presentation on any six endangered species, covering different regions of the world.
Your presentation should have the following points:

- details about the animals: natural habitat, the previous and current count
- factors responsible for the loss in numbers
- organizations/programs/sanctuaries involved in awareness and rescue operations
- measures undertaken to ensure that they do not become extinct

Now I can... **Self-Assessment**

- o read and appreciate a poem on the beauty of an animal in its natural habitat.
- o understand and identify imagery.
- o make a presentation.

Read at Leisure

The Eagle: This short poem by Alfred Lord Tennyson describes the eagle as a majestic bird who surveys the world beneath him from a great height.

How to Know the Wild Animals: This humorous poem by Carolyn Wells suggests some unusual ways to identify various wild animals.

VI

Community and Neighbourhood

Take Off

A. Circle the elements that you feel are important to build a thriving community. Then write them in the suitable columns.

factory	school	hospital	stadium	housing
water tank	beauty salon	movie theatre	college	transport system
crèche	university	gym	park	sanctuary
mall/market	swimming pool	playground	office	restaurants
roads	community centre			

Education	Environment	Entertainment	Others

B. Anything which disturbs our natural environment can cause pollution. The major types of pollution are air pollution, water pollution, soil pollution, light pollution, and noise pollution. Look at the types of polluting substances listed here. Identify the type of pollution each group causes.

1. Fumes from transport and factories, burning fossil fuels: ________
2. Untreated sewage, factory waste, oil spills and plastic: ________
3. Traffic sounds, machinery sounds, loudspeakers: ________
4. Billboard lights, floodlights, over-illumination: ________
5. Landfills, mining, intensive farming: ________

parable

11 A Spark Neglected Burns the House

Leo Tolstoy

Reading

Have you heard of the saying, 'an eye for an eye makes the whole world blind'? Read a story that narrates what happens to two men who are unwilling to forgive and forget.

There once lived in a village a **peasant** named Ivan. He had a wife and three sons. The eldest was married, the second about to marry, and the third was a big lad who could mind the horses by himself. Ivan took care of his old father, who had been lying ill on top of the brick oven for seven years.

Ivan had all he needed: three horses and a colt, a cow with a calf, and fifteen sheep. The women made all the clothing for the family, besides helping in the fields, and the men **tilled** the land. They always had enough grain to last beyond the next harvest and sold enough oats to pay the taxes and meet their other needs.

Food for thought

The Russian oven or stove is a type of brick stove usually built in the middle of a log cottage. It was used both for cooking as well as heating up the room. In the severe Russian winters, it was quite common for people to sleep on top of the oven to keep warm.

Ivan and his children might have lived on happily had it not been for a **feud** between him and his next-door neighbour, Limping Gabriel.

List the animals that Ivan had.

It all began about a **trifle**. Ivan's daughter-in-law had a hen that began laying rather early in the season, and she started collecting its eggs for Easter. One day, the hen, probably frightened by the children, flew across the fence into the neighbour's yard and laid its egg there. The woman heard the cackling but said to herself: 'I have no time now; I must tidy up for Sunday. I'll fetch the egg later.' In the evening, she went to the coop but found no egg. She asked her brother-in-law whether he had taken the egg. 'No,' he replied, 'your hen laid its egg in the neighbour's yard. It was there she was cackling, and she flew back across the fence from there.'

The woman went to the neighbour's house. Gabriel's mother came out to meet her.

'What do you want, young woman?'

'Granny, my hen flew across this morning. Did she not lay an egg here?'

'We never saw anything. The Lord be thanked, our own hens started laying long ago. We have no need of other people's! And we don't go looking for eggs in other people's yards, **lass**!'

peasant: farmer
tilled: ploughed
feud: long and bitter dispute between two families, clans or people
trifle: an unimportant matter
lass: a young girl

The young woman felt angry and replied in harsher tones than she should have. Soon, the women were quarrelling with each other.

'You're a thief!'

'You're starving your old father-in-law to death!'

'You're a good-for-nothing!'

'You've made a hole in the **sieve** I lent you!'

'It's our **yoke** you're carrying your pails on—you give back our yoke right now!'

They snatched off one another's shawls and began fighting. Gabriel, returning from the fields, stopped to take his mother's side. Ivan and his son too joined in. Ivan was a strong fellow. He scattered the whole lot of them and pulled a handful of hair out of Gabriel's beard. People came to see what the matter was, and the fighters were separated with difficulty.

Soon, not a day passed without a quarrel between the families. The children, too, fought with one another, having learnt to do so from their elders.

The old man, from where he lay on top of the oven, tried to **persuade** them to make peace, but they would not listen. He told them, 'It's a foolish thing, picking quarrels about such a **paltry** matter. The whole thing began with an egg. It doesn't matter who took it. Doesn't God send enough for all? If you nurse your anger, it will only make things worse.'

But the younger folk would not listen to him. At first the peasants only **slandered** one another; but soon, life became harder for them as they kept **suing** one another at the village assembly, and before the Justice of the Peace until all the judges were tired of them.

In the seventh year, at a wedding, Ivan's son accused Gabriel of horse stealing. Gabriel was unable to **contain** his anger and gave the man a blow that **laid** him **up** in bed for a week. Ivan immediately went to the magistrate to **lodge** a complaint.

What was the punishment given by the magistrate?

'How dare Gabriel hurt my son? He won't escape imprisonment, or **exile** to Siberia.'

But the son recovered soon and was up and about. The magistrate gave Gabriel a **hefty** fine, but neither imprisoned him nor sent him to Siberia. Dissatisfied, Ivan **bribed** the clerk and got Gabriel sentenced to receive twenty **lashes** with a birch rod at the district court.

When the sentence was read, Gabriel grew as pale as a sheet, turned around and went out into the passage.

sieve: a strainer
yoke: a device for joining together two draft animals
persuade: urge somebody to do something
paltry: unimportant, worthless
slandered: spread malicious lies and rumours
suing: starting legal proceedings
contain: control, restrain
laid up: to be bedridden
lodge: bring a formal charge against someone
exile: banishment
hefty: large
bribed: influenced with money or gifts
lashes: whip strokes

Ivan followed him and overheard him say, 'Very well! He will have me **flogged:** that will make it burn; but something of his own may burn worse than that!'

Gabriel wished to say something more but his lips **quivered**, and he turned towards the wall. Even the officials were frightened by his looks. 'He will do mischief to himself or to his neighbour,' they thought.

When Ivan reached home, he remembered how Gabriel had listened to the **sentence**, and how he had turned to the wall. His heart grew heavy. He thought how he himself would feel if he were sentenced, and he pitied Gabriel. His father, who had dragged himself with difficulty to sit with his son, shook his head when he heard of Gabriel's sentence.

'You are doing wrong, Ivan!' said he. 'It's very bad— not for him so much as for yourself! They'll flog him: but will that do you any good?'

'He'll not do it again,' said Ivan.

'What is it he'll not do again? What has he done worse than you?'

'Why, think of the harm he has done me!' said Ivan. 'He nearly killed my daughter-in-law, and now he's threatening to burn us up. Am I to thank him for it?'

The old man sighed, and said: 'Ah, lad! **Malice** blinds you. Others' sins are before your eyes, but your own are behind your back. It's not the way I used to live, lad, and it's not the way I taught you. How did his old father and I live? Why, as neighbours should! If someone **offends** you, forgive him. Then life will be easy, and your heart will always be light.'

His father's words rang true to Ivan. He decided to make peace with Gabriel. But soon, everyone came home talking of the sentencing and discussing a new row they had had with Gabriel's household. Hearing them, Ivan's heart grew cold again. By nightfall, he had quite forgotten his father's advice.

Walking back home from his evening **chores** around the **homestead**, he heard Gabriel across the fence, muttering **hoarsely** to himself, 'He deserves his fate. What on earth is he good for?'

Ivan was alarmed. 'I'll just walk around the buildings to make sure everything is safe. Who can tell what he's after?' he thought.

When did Ivan hear Gabriel?

Stepping into the street, he reached a corner and looked along the fence. Someone quickly came out and disappeared again. Ivan stopped and stood quietly, listening and looking. Everything was still; only the leaves of the willows fluttered in

flogged: whipped
quivered: trembled
sentence: punishment
malice: evil intention
offends: to anger, annoy
alarmed: worried
chores: routine tasks
homestead: a dwelling with lands and buildings
hoarsely: roughly

the wind, and the straws of the **thatch** rustled. At first it seemed **pitch dark**, but when his eyes got used to the darkness, he could see the far corner, where a plough lay. Suddenly, something flared up brightly, and he saw a man **crouching**, with his back towards him, lighting a bunch of straw. In minutes, the flames were reaching up to the roof, and, standing beneath it, Gabriel was clearly visible.

Like a hawk **swooping** down on a **lark**[1], Ivan rushed at Gabriel. 'Now I'll catch him!'

At Gabriel's own gate, Ivan was about to seize him, when something struck him a **stunning** blow, quite **deafening** him. It was Gabriel, who had picked up an oak **wedge** and hit him with it.

When Ivan came to his senses some time later, his homestead was burning. It roared and crackled like an engine at work.

'What is this, friends?' cried Ivan, **bewildered** and disbelieving, 'All I had to do was snatch it out from under the **eaves** and trample on it!'

Ivan tried to shout but his breath failed him.

He wanted to run but his legs would not obey him. The flames were now leaping out of the hut. The family barely managed to save the old father; and they escaped in what they had on. Everything else except the horses and cattle were lost.

What did Gabriel hit Ivan with?

Gabriel's house also caught fire. Then, the wind rising, the flames spread to the other side of the street and soon, half the village was burnt down.

The fire raged all night. When morning came, Ivan's father lay dying. Burning **embers** had fallen on him and injured him. He sent for his son.

'Ivan,' said the old man **feebly**, when he saw Ivan, 'Now, before God, say whose is the sin? What did I tell you?'

Only then did Ivan come to his senses.

'Mine, father!' he cried.

He fell on his knees, crying, 'Forgive me, father; I am guilty before you and before God. I don't know how we are to live now! What are we to do?'

'You'll manage, Ivan,' whispered his father. 'Don't tell anyone who started the fire! Hide another man's sin, and God will forgive two of yours!' And the old man sighed, stretched out, and died.

Literary term

1. This is a **simile**, where Ivan's rushing movement at Gabriel is compared to the ferocity of a hawk's flight to catch a lark.

---

thatch: roof made of straw or leaves
pitch dark: very dark
crouching: bending or stooping
swooping: swiftly attacking
lark: a small brown bird
stunning: (here) extremely surprising or shocking
deafening: (here) almost making deaf
wedge: chunk
bewildered: confused
eaves: overhanging lower edges of a roof
embers: the burning remains of a fire
feebly: weakly

When the villagers began rebuilding, Ivan did not tell anyone what he had seen that night. Gabriel wondered why. At first he felt afraid, but after a while he got used to it. The men left off quarrelling, and then their families left off too. They lived as good neighbours should. Ivan remembered his old father's teaching: to **quench** a fire at the first spark. If anyone did him an injury, he tried not to **avenge** himself, but rather to set matters right again. And so, he got back on his feet again and lived better than he ever had before.

quench: (here) put out

avenge: get even

Common idioms and proverbs

turn the other cheek: This idiom means to remain calm and not act in an aggressive way when somebody has hurt or angered you. It signifies what Ivan's father advised him to do.

Example: I usually *turn the other cheek* when someone is rude to me.

About the author

Leo Tolstoy (1828–1910) was a Russian writer, considered to be one of the greatest writers of all time. He was nominated for the Nobel Prize multiple times. He wrote short stories, children's books, and books for young adults, usually upholding moral or life lessons. His famous novels *War and Peace* and *Anna Karenina* have been read and loved by people all over the world.

Comprehension

A. Answer the questions.

1. Did Ivan's family have enough for their needs? Give reasons for your answer.
2. Why did life become harder for the two families after the first row?
3. Why did Ivan go to the magistrate to lodge a complaint? Why do you think the magistrate didn't give Gabriel a harsh sentence?
4. Why did Ivan pity Gabriel and when did he do so?
5. What did Ivan see in the pitch darkness? What happened immediately after that?
6. Why didn't Ivan tell anyone what he had seen that night? What good thing happened as a result?
7. Ivan's father gave him advice thrice in the story. What were they?

B. Answer the questions with reference to context.

1. *'...And we don't go looking for eggs in other people's yards, lass!'*
   a. Who said these words and to whom?
   b. Why had the person spoken to gone 'looking for eggs in other people's yards'?
   c. How did the quarrel start? What happened when the others joined in?

2. *When the sentence was read, Gabriel grew as pale as a sheet, turned around and went out into the passage.*
   a. Who was Gabriel and what sentence did he receive?
   b. Why did Gabriel grow pale? What did he do then?
   c. Who overheard him, and what were their reactions?

3. *'All I had to do was snatch it out from under the eaves and trample on it!'*
   a. Who said these words? Why did it seem that he was surprised?
   b. What is referred to here as 'it'? Why did the speaker want to trample on 'it'?
   c. What happened as a result of the speaker's failure to do what he had planned?

Life Skills and Values — compassion, forgiveness

1. What lesson does this story teach us?
2. Explain these lines: 'Malice blinds you. Others' sins are before your eyes, but your own are behind your back.'
3. Do you think it is necessary to 'get even' when someone hurts you? Why?

Vocabulary

synonyms

A. Words like *quarrel* and *row* have the same meaning, and are therefore, synonyms. Choose the correct synonym for the underlined word in each sentence.

1. The farmer <u>tilled</u> the soil for a livelihood.
   a. watered ☐ b. ploughed ☑ c. covered ☐
2. The teacher <u>persuaded</u> her class to finish the assignment on time.
   a. assured ☐ b. challenged ☐ c. convinced ☐
3. The baby's lips <u>quivered</u> and she broke into tears.
   a. curled ☐ b. pursed ☐ c. trembled ☐
4. One should not bear <u>malice</u> towards one's neighbours.
   a. hatred ☐ b. patience ☐ c. trust ☐
5. His mother was <u>alarmed</u> when she got a call from the school suddenly.
   a. happy ☐ b. worried ☐ c. relaxed ☐
6. The sign read 'Do not <u>trample</u> the flowers'.
   a. squash ☐ b. pet ☐ c. cut ☐
7. Grandma was <u>bewildered</u> to see the entire family leave the table hurriedly.
   a. excited ☐ b. saddened ☐ c. confused ☐

proverbs

B. Match the proverbs in Column A with their meanings in Column B. Then make sentences of your own with any three of them.

Column A	Column B
1. Don't judge a book by its cover.	a. Worry about a problem when it actually happens.
2. Too many cooks spoil the broth.	b. Rely on one particular course of action for success.
3. Cross that bridge when you come to it.	c. Tell a secret carelessly or by mistake.
4. Look before you leap.	d. If too many people are involved in doing something, it will not be done well.
5. Let the cat out of the bag.	e. Do not form an opinion about somebody/something from their appearance only.
6. Put all your eggs in one basket.	f. Think about the possible results or dangers of something before doing it.

Grammar

correlative conjunctions

Read these sentences.

The magistrate did not imprison Gabriel. He did not send Gabriel to Siberia.
The magistrate **neither** imprisoned Gabriel **nor** sent him to Siberia.

Notice that the two sentences have been joined by the conjunctions *neither … nor*. They are correlative conjunctions.

Correlative conjunctions are conjunctions that connect two or more statements or words of equal importance.

Some common correlative conjunctions are *not only... but also, either... or, although... yet, no sooner... than, hardly... when*, and *whether... or*.

A. Join these pairs of sentences with the correlative conjunctions given in the box. You may have to make other necessary changes.

both...and	hardly...when	neither...nor	whether...or
although...yet	either...or	not only...but also	

1. It began to rain. The band started playing.
2. Rik is an excellent swimmer. Isha is an excellent swimmer.

3. I don't know if this coat is for her brother. I don't know if this coat is for her sister.
4. Cynthia is not present in class. Joanna is not present in class.
5. Rita had injured her knee. She did not cry.
6. Piya can have the orange. Piya can have the apple.
7. Mehul was chosen for the football team. He was made the captain of the team.

types of phrases

A phrase is a group of words which conveys some meaning but does not make complete sense. It does not have a finite verb or a subject of its own. Phrases are of the following types:

An **adjective phrase** is a group of words that performs the function of an adjective in a sentence.

Example: Ivan was a man **of great strength**.

An **adverb phrase** is a group of words that acts as an adverb in a sentence.

Example: Ivan's daughter-in-law spoke to the old lady **in a harsh manner**.

A **noun phrase** is a group of words that acts as a noun in a sentence. It can function both as a subject or an object.

Example: **The leaves of the willows** fluttered in the wind.

B. Underline the phrases in these sentences and identify their types.

1. Riya proudly displayed her fan from Japan.
2. The lady drank the cup of coffee in a hurried manner.
3. Virat Kohli is a cricketer by profession.
4. The Kumar family spent a day filled with enjoyment at the amusement park.
5. The thief denied stealing the car.
6. The student answered all the questions with confidence.
7. Caring for animals comes quite naturally to her.
8. Varun left home at an early hour.

C. Rewrite the sentences replacing the adjective and adverb phrases with suitable adjectives or adverbs. One is done for you.

1. Our principal is a man *of honour*.
   Our principal is an honourable man.
2. This mobile phone is *of no use* as it keeps switching off.
3. Nobody likes to have a roommate *with such short temper*.

4. The king wore a coat *made of silk*.
5. We walked out of the cinema hall *in silence*.
6. Parul had wrapped these gifts *with a lot of patience*.
7. Every item in this shop is *made by hand*.
8. The car sped away from the police jeep *with great swiftness*.

Study Skills

Spelling

words with *-ary*, *-ery* and *-ory*

Words that end with *-ary*, *-ery* and *-ory* are often misspelt.
Look at the following table which shows some words that end with the three suffixes and are often spelt wrong.

Words ending with *-ary*	Words ending with *-ery*	Words ending with *-ory*
imaginary	bakery	preparatory
secondary	misery	category
necessary	eatery	explanatory

Fill in the blanks with the correct words.

1. The ______________ (discovery/discovary) of penicillin was a significant step in medicine.
2. The ______________ (secretory/secretary) reminded her boss about the meeting.
3. The cricket ______________ (commentery/commentary) kept us glued to the radio.
4. Her allergy made her eyes red and ______________ (watary/watery).
5. We will be studying about the ______________ (respiratery/respiratory) system today.
6. The cook prepared a ______________ (satisfactary/satisfactory) meal for the guests.

Listening

listening for information

Listen to a news report and complete the sentences.

1. Since mid-December, cold wave conditions have continued in ______________.
2. The day temperatures remain ______________.
3. ______________ have added to the cold conditions.
4. The Meteorological Department has said ______________.
5. ______________ are being urged to seek shelter in ______________.
6. The Indian Red Cross has set up ______________.
7. The city helpline number is being manned ______________.

Speaking

role play: expressing emotions

Imagine that a new student has joined your class. You find that your best friend spends most of her time with her. How would you feel in such a situation? Would you feel jealousy or anger? How would you discuss and resolve the situation? Enact a dialogue with your partner on the topic. You may start like this:

You: Hi Neha, can we talk for sometime?

Neha: Oh, sure! What's the matter? Why do you look so serious?

Useful words and phrases

- Can we...
- I think you...
- Couldn't we both...
- Let's all be...

Writing

writing a letter expressing regret

Imagine that you are Gabriel. Write a letter to your neighbour Ivan expressing regret for the way you behaved with him. Explain your reasons for doing so and express your gratitude to Ivan for not blaming you for starting the fire.
You may include the following points in your letter.

- apology for the things you had done
- feelings of regret and shame
- hope for forgiveness

Self-Assessment

Now I can...

- read and understand a story with a moral.
- understand and use synonyms and proverbs.
- use correlative conjunctions to join sentences, and identify and use the different types of phrases.
- express emotions suited to a given situation.
- write a letter expressing regret.

Read at Leisure

The Hitopadesha: This collection of fables, translated from the original Sanskrit by G. L. Chandiramani, imparts worldly wisdom and advice for living as a useful member of society.

George's Secret Key to the Universe: This book by Lucy and Stephen Hawking is a fast-paced adventure of a young boy who accidentally lands up in the world of his eccentric neighbours.

light verse

12 The People Upstairs

Ogden Nash

Reading

Do you have noisy neighbours? How do you or your family deal with them? Read this poem to find out what the poet feels about the people living above his flat.

The people upstairs all practise ballet[1]
Their living room is a **bowling alley**
Their bedroom is full of **conducted tours**.
Their radio is louder than yours,
They celebrate weekends all the week.
When they take a shower, your ceilings leak.
They try to get their parties to mix
By supplying their guests with **Pogo sticks**,
And when their fun at last **abates**,
They go to the bathroom on roller skates.
I would love the people upstairs wondrous
If instead of above us, they just lived under us.

bowling alley: a long narrow wooden lane down which the ball is rolled in bowling

conducted tours: guided visits to see something or someplace of interest

Pogo sticks: poles with a bar to stand on and a spring at the bottom, that one jumps around on for fun

abates: reduces, lessens

Literary term

1. This is a **metaphor**. The poet compares the racket made by the tenants upstairs to the noise made by ballet dancers when they practise.

About the poet

Ogden Nash (1902–1971) was an American writer of humorous and witty poetry. He wrote about ordinary problems of daily life using quirky rhymes. Some of his well-known books are *The Tale of Custard the Dragon*, *Ogden Nash's Zoo* and *Adventures of Isabel.*

Understanding the poem

A. Look at the pictures and answer the questions related to them.

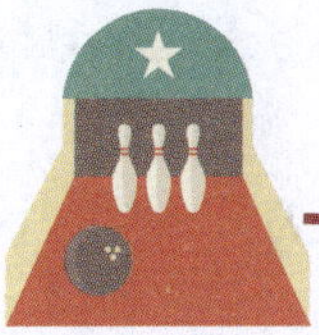

1. Which sound is heard before this?

____

____

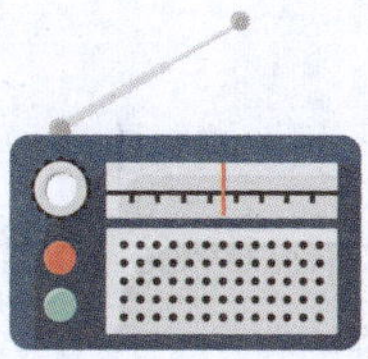

2. What is said about the radio?

____

____

3. What happens after the weekend?

____

____

4. Where do they go wearing skates?

____

____

B. Answer the questions with reference to context.

1. *Their living room is a bowling alley…*
   a. Whose living room is a bowling alley?
   b. Why is the room being described in this manner? What figure of speech is it?
   c. What, according to the poet, do they practise?
2. *They try to get their parties to mix…*
   a. Who are being referred to as 'they'?
   b. What does the phrase, 'parties to mix' mean? How do 'they' try to do that?
   c. Do you think this action disturbs the poet?
3. *I would love the people upstairs wondrous.*
   a. Who is 'I' here?
   b. What would make the speaker love the people upstairs? What do you understand by the term 'wondrous' here?
   c. What does this tell us about his feelings for his neighbours?

Life Skills and Values

being a good neighbour

1. What are the qualities that one expects in a neighbour?
2. The poet is quite annoyed with his noisy neighbours. However, living in a community can also be beneficial. Think and list three such benefits.
3. Did you find the poem humorous? Give some examples from the poem.
4. 'Their bedroom is full of conducted tours.../They celebrate weekends all the week.../They go to the bathroom on roller skates.' What does the poet mean by these statements? Explain in your own words.

Vocabulary

-ing adjectives

We often use *-ing* words as adjectives to describe a noun. These are formed by adding the suffix *-ing* to verbs.

Examples: Their **living** room is a **bowling** alley.

A. Fill in the blanks with suitable adjectives formed from the words in the box.

annoy	strike	shock	bore	bark	amuse

1. Raghu has an ______________ habit of interrupting people when they are talking.
2. The ______________ dog disturbed everyone last night.
3. The film was so ______________ that we left at the interval.
4. The ______________ natural rock formations in the park attract tourists.
5. I do not find these stories ______________.
6. Everyone stopped what they were doing after hearing the ______________ news.

rhyme scheme

B. The rhyme scheme is the pattern of rhymes at the end of each line of a poem or song. Write the rhyme scheme of these verses.

1. They try to get their parties to mix ☐
By supplying their guests with Pogo sticks ☐
And when their fun at last abates, ☐
They go to the bathroom on roller skates. ☐
I would love the people upstairs wondrous ☐
If instead of above us, they just lived under us. ☐

2. Little Jack Horner
Sat in the corner,
Eating a Christmas pie;
He put in his thumb,
And pulled out a plum,
And said, 'What a good boy am I!'

Activity

describing situations using figurative language

Look at this sentence.

The people upstairs all practise ballet.

Here, the poet describes the noise made by the people upstairs by comparing it to the sounds made by the quick movements of ballet dancers.

We often use figurative language to describe common or everyday occurrences as something grand, strange and unusual.

Look at some situations related to a scene at the end of a school day. Work in groups and discuss what each of these situations can be compared to. Then write a paragraph describing them, using figurative language.

- noisy classroom: I felt as if I was sitting in the middle of a busy street, with cars honking and people talking all around me.
- an interesting English lesson
- hot weather
- teacher teaching patiently
- wait for the final bell to ring

Self-Assessment

Now I can...

- o read and enjoy a humorous poem about noisy neighbours.
- o use *-ing* adjectives and identify rhyme scheme patterns.
- o describe situations using figurative language.

Read at Leisure

Neighbours: This poem by Rudyard Kipling lists the qualities of a good and a bad neighbour, and what life has in offer for each.

The Stick-Together Families: This poem by Edgar Guest talks about the virtues of families who understand the importance of staying together.

Project 2

A. You read about Schatz's illness, symptoms and his path to recovery in the chapter *A Day's Wait*. Look at the names of some common diseases in the following table. Working in groups of four, find out more information about them and complete the health chart.

Name of Illness	Causes	Symptoms	Preventive Measures (if any)
1. Typhoid			
2. Influenza			
3. Measles			
4. Chicken pox			
5. Mumps			

Based on what you found out, have a discussion in class on these topics.

1. **Does less pollution promote good health? How?**
2. **Four habits that promote good health and reduce the risk of falling ill.**

B. You read about scorpions and their habits in the chapter *An Unexpected Guest*. Work in pairs and collect information about geckos. Create a scrapbook on them and include the following information. Add pictures of various species of geckos as well.

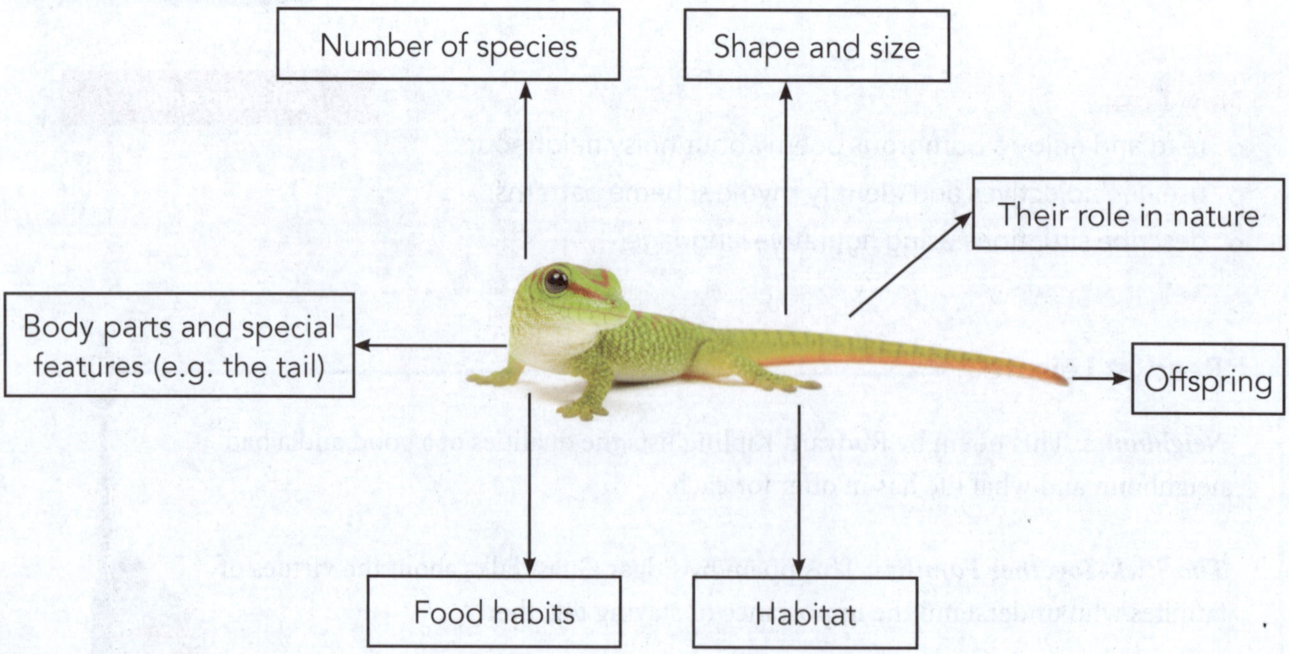

VII

Food and Celebrations

Take Off

A. We celebrate various festivals with our friends and family. Read these sentences and identify the Indian festivals.

1. We decorate our homes with lights and share sweets with our friends on ______________
2. ______________ is a festival when we play with colours to celebrate spring's arrival.
3. During ______________, we watch Ramlila performances and Ravana's effigies are burnt.
4. On ______________, children get *eidi* from parents.
5. On ______________, children go on treasure hunts for chocolate eggs and bunnies.
6. During ______________, boat races are held in Kerala.
7. To celebrate their bond, a sister ties a thread on her brother's wrist on ______________
8. ______________ marks the end of winter, and is celebrated with bonfires, singing and dancing, in North Indian states.

B. Yorkshire Pudding and Brussels sprouts are two examples of food items named after places. Complete the names of the following food items.

1. Waldorf ______________
2. Bombay ______________
3. ______________ Chettinad
4. Bourbon ______________
5. ______________ toast
6. ______________ delight
7. Malabar ______________
8. Black ______________ cake

(The answers are given at the end of the unit.)

mystery

13 The Theft of the Ruby

Agatha Christie

Reading

Imagine your family was celebrating a festive occasion, and amidst the gaiety, you find yourself caught in a mystery. Read on to find out what might happen next.

A band of young people were chatting **companionably** together, while the big logs crackled merrily in the fireplace. Old Miss Endicott, known as Aunt Emily, looked on fondly at Jean, Nancy Cardell, the two younger boys, Johnson and Eric, their friend Charlie Pease, and Evelyn Haworth. Evelyn was engaged to Oscar Levering, who was also visiting with his sister. Then her eyes wandered to her eldest nephew, Roger, who sat **morosely** silent, looking at Evelyn.

Food for thought

Hercule Poirot, a fictional Belgian detective, is one of the most famous characters created by Agatha Christie. Poirot is said to have left Belgium for England as a refugee during World War I. He is supported in many cases by his friend, Captain Arthur Hastings. He is known for using 'the little grey cells' and 'order and method' while solving cases.

Seated among them was a little man with a curious egg-shaped head and fierce **upstanding** moustaches.

The famous detective Hercule Poirot had joined them for Christmas.

'Real Christmas weather!' cried Johnnie, looking out of the window.

'Let's make a snowman!' suggested Jean.

They all disappeared like a **whirlwind**[1].

Poirot noticed that Evelyn was staring at the fire, twisting a ring on her left hand. She hadn't gone out with the rest.

'You seem lost, madam,' said Poirot gently.

'I am so miserable, Mr Poirot,' she answered. A year ago, Evelyn Haworth's mother had fallen seriously ill and needed an expensive operation. Desperate and without money, Evelyn had accepted Mr Levering's marriage proposal.

companionably: in a friendly way
morosely: gloomily
upstanding: straight, upright
whirlwind: a very strong wind that moves fast in a spinning movement

Literary term

1. This is an example of a **simile**, where the rapidity with which the people disappeared is compared to the movement of a whirlwind, which also comes and disappears very fast.

'Mr Levering kept his word. The operation was performed and my mother is now well and strong again; and I – I am to marry Mr Levering after Christmas.'

'I see,' said Mr Poirot. 'But Roger also cared for you. And now he has come home to find his dream shattered.'

Evelyn didn't reply, but did not disagree.

At that moment, the door opened. Mr Levering stood on the threshold.

'Come out for a **stroll**, Evelyn,' he said.

She rose **listlessly**.

Poirot asked politely: 'Madam Levering, she is still unwell?'

'Yes, I'm sorry to say that my sister is still in bed.'

In the snow-covered grounds, Levering and Evelyn met the others.

'What do you think of the great detective, Evelyn?' Jean cried out.

'We have a real detective in the house!' said Charlie, 'I wish there could be a murder, too.'

'I've got an idea,' cried Jean. 'Let's enact a murder – a **spoof**, I mean.'

Five voices began to talk at once about the plan.

'We can use red paint.'

'Nancy can be it; she's got those **scarlet** pyjamas.'

'Let's ask Graves for some paint.'

The group **stampeded** back to the house.

Back inside, Levering asked Roger, 'Why so **glum**, Endicott?'

'I was just wondering,' he said quietly, 'what brings Mr Poirot here.'

Levering seemed **taken aback**; but at that moment the big gong rang, and everybody went in for Christmas dinner. The **Squire**, Aunt Emily's brother, **carved** rapidly, and everyone fell on the **turkey**. Graves, the butler, appeared, bearing aloft a gigantic plum pudding, **wreathed** in flames. A **hullabaloo** broke out.

'Quick, my piece is going out. **Buck up**, Graves; unless it's still burning, I shan't get my wish.'

Suddenly the Squire's face became purple and his hand went to his mouth.

Food for thought

Plum pudding was originally made with plums. Nowadays, the pudding is made with raisins, but the name has not changed. This pudding is especially made for Christmas, and as part of the tradition, every member of the family gets to stir the pudding when it is being made and make a wish.

stroll: walk
listlessly: not in an enthusiastic manner
spoof: a trick played on someone as a joke
scarlet: bright red
stampeded: rushed
glum: sad
taken aback: surprised
Squire: a man of high social position, a chief landowner
carved: (here) cut a large piece of cooked meat into smaller pieces
turkey: a large bird, popular food on festive days like Christmas
wreathed: surrounded
hullabaloo: loud noise and confusion
buck up: hurry up

'Emily!' he roared. 'Why do you let the cook put glass in the puddings?'

'Glass?' cried Miss Endicott, astonished.

The Squire dropped the piece of glass into a small **finger bowl** of water, placed there for the **sixpences** and other trinkets found in the **trifle**. He rinsed it and held it up.

Mr Poirot took it from him and examined it attentively. It was a big red stone, the colour of a ruby.

'Is it real? A ruby that size would be worth thousands, wouldn't it, Mr Poirot?' said Jean.

'But how did it get into the pudding?' asked Miss Endicott.

After dinner, Poirot paid a visit to the cook and found that the pudding had been made three days ago. Everyone had come out into the kitchen to have a stir and wish, an old custom. But this wasn't the Christmas pudding, which was always boiled in a **china** mould with **holly leaves**. However, today the kitchen maid accidentally broke the mould, with the pudding in it. So, the one in the aluminium dish was served instead. Mr Poirot thanked the cook for this information and left, smiling a little to himself. The fingers of his right hand played with something in his pocket.

'Mr Poirot! Do wake up! Something dreadful has happened!' screamed Johnnie the following morning. Mr Poirot arose, and followed Johnnie down the stairs. Everyone was **clustered** around the door into the garden. Jean came forward and pointed dramatically through the open door. The snow-covered landscape looked ghostly in the early dawn except for a splash of **vivid** scarlet. Nancy Cardell lay motionless on the snow, clad in scarlet silk pyjamas. From her left side rose the **hilt** of a dagger.

Poirot went out into the snow. But he didn't go directly to the girl. He followed the footprints – of a man and a woman – that led to the spot. The man's footprints went away in the opposite direction, alone. Poirot stood on the path, **reflectively**. Suddenly Mr Levering burst out of the house.

'Good God!' he cried excitedly. 'What's this?'

---

finger bowl: a small bowl containing water for rinsing the fingers after meal

sixpences: small silver coins, used in Britain till 1971

trifle: a dessert made of layers of sponge cake, jelly, fruit and custard, and usually covered with cream

china: (here) porcelain or ceramic

holly leaves: leaves of an evergreen shrub usually used during Christmas for decoration

clustered: grouped together

vivid: bright

hilt: handle

reflectively: thoughtfully

‘It looks,’ said Mr Poirot **grimly**, ‘like murder. You must send for the police.’

There was a pause, and then Johnnie came forward.

‘Mr Poirot, I hope you won’t be too mad with us. It’s all a joke, you know,’ he declared. ‘Say Nancy, get up! Don’t lie there all day.’

But the figure on the ground did not move. Suddenly a feeling of dread came over the boy. Poirot strode over the snow, waving the others back. The boy followed him, frightened. Poirot knelt down by the girl and **signed** to Johnnie.

‘Feel her hand and pulse.’

Johnnie bent forward. Nancy’s hand had gone stiff and cold, and no pulse was to be found.

‘She’s dead!’ he gasped. ‘But how? Why?’

‘I wonder,’ Mr Poirot said **musingly**. Suddenly he **unclasped** her other hand. They uttered an exclamation. In Nancy’s palm was a red stone that winked and flashed forth fire.

Mr Poirot quickly put his hand into his pocket, and came away empty.

‘The ruby,’ said Johnnie. Then, as Mr Poirot bent to examine the dagger, and the stained snow, he cried out, ‘Surely it can’t be blood, Mr Poirot. It’s only paint.’

‘You are right,’ he said quietly. It’s only paint. Now, did she eat or drink anything this morning?’

‘She had a cup of tea,’ said the boy. ‘Mr Levering made it for her. He’s got a **spirit lamp** in his room.’

‘Such a handy thing,’ Mr Levering answered. ‘My sister’s been glad of it this visit. There’s no need to worry the servants all the time.’

At that moment, Mr Poirot’s eyes fell to Mr Levering’s feet. He was wearing carpet slippers.

‘You have changed your boots, I see,’ he said. Levering stared at him. ‘Now, for the police.’

‘I’ll go,’ cried Levering. ‘It won’t take me a minute to put my boots on.’

He disappeared into the house.

‘Until the police come, nothing here must be touched. Shall we go inside? I have a little history to **recount** to you.’ said Mr Poirot.

‘A precious ruby once belonged to a very celebrated man. He came to London, where he met a pretty young lady. Soon after, the lady disappeared with a historic ruby which had belonged to his family for generations. This man came to me. “Recover for me my ruby,” he says. I know that this lady has a brother, and together they have tricked many people. I know where they are staying for Christmas.

By the kindness of Mr Endicott, I too become a guest there. But when this lady hears that I am arriving, she is alarmed. She knows that I am after the ruby. She needs to hide it immediately in a safe place; and where but in a plum-pudding! She is stirring with the rest, you see, and she pops it into a pudding bowl of aluminium that is different from the others. By a strange chance, that pudding came to be used on Christmas Day.’

The tragedy forgotten for the moment, everyone stared at him open-mouthed. Evelyn rose with a cry, her eyes fixed on Poirot.

grimly: very seriously

signed: (here) called by using a hand movement

musingly: with a lot of thought

unclasped: loosened the grip

spirit lamp: a lamp that burns spirits instead of oil

recount: tell somebody about something

The detective continued, 'I expect that Mr Levering and his sister will not return.'

'Did he kill Nancy?' whispered Jean.

Poirot rose, walking back to the scene of the crime.

But when the others reached the spot, they gasped. The snow was smooth and unbroken.

'Most extraordinary,' said Mr Poirot, '*The Mystery of the Disappearing Body*.' His eyes twinkled gently.

Jean came up to him in sudden suspicion.

'Mr Poirot, you have been spoofing us all the time, haven't you?'

'I knew about your little plot,' Mr Poirot smiled, 'and so arranged a little **counterplot** of my own. Ah, here is Nancy.'

Nancy Cardell appeared, her eyes shining.

'I asked **Mademoiselle** Nancy to act a part for me. She persuaded Mr Levering to make her a cup of tea, and managed that he should be the one chosen to leave footprints on the snow. So when the time came, and he thought that she was really dead, I could frighten him with it.'

'After everyone went inside,' Nancy began, 'he came down with his sister, snatched the ruby out of my hand, and off they went **post-haste**. Goodness Mr Poirot, my arm hurts still after that **tourniquet** you made me put on it.'

'So the ruby is lost?' cried Eric.

'Feel in my left pocket.'

Jean thrust in an eager hand, and drew it out again with a squeal of triumph. The great ruby in its crimson splendour
was there for all to see.

'You see,' smiled Poirot, 'the other was a **paste replica** I had brought with me from London.'

counterplot: a plot or plan to prevent another plan from working

Mademoiselle: Miss, in French

post-haste: with great speed

tourniquet: a strip of cloth usually tied tightly round a limb to control the circulation of blood to some part of the body or stop the flow of blood a substance like glass, used for making artificial jewels

replica: an exact copy

About the author

Agatha Christie (1890–1976) was an English writer, celebrated for her thrillers and murder mysteries. Her stories usually revolve around her fictional detectives, Hercule Poirot and Miss Marple. She also wrote the world's longest-running play, a murder mystery, *The Mousetrap*. *Murder on the Orient Express*, and *And Then There Were None* are some of her famous novels, which have been made into films and television series.

Comprehension

A. Complete the flow chart to show the sequence of events in the story.

A group of people had gathered for Christmas celebrations including the famous __________.

→ The young people were excited and decided __________ __________.

→ At dinner, the plum pudding was brought in, but then the Squire discovered __________.

→ The cook informed Poirot that the original pudding __________ __________.

→ Next morning, they found __________, lying dead in the snow. Poirot noticed __________.

→ Johnnie realized that instead of acting, __________ __________.

→ They found the __________ in her hand which Poirot __________. Mr Levering offered to __________.

→ Poirot told everyone that __________ __________ __________ __________.

→ It was also revealed that Nancy was __________ and the ruby __________ __________ __________.

B. Answer the questions with reference to context.

1. *'Emily!' he roared. 'Why do you let the cook put glass in the puddings?'*
   a. Who said these words and to whom?
   b. Describe the scene at the dinner table prior to this.
   c. Why did the speaker roar? What had happened to him?
   d. What was the 'glass' that is spoken about?

2. *'She's dead!' he gasped. 'But how? Why?'*
   a. Who said these words and to whom?
   b. Who was 'dead'? How did they check to see if she was 'dead'?
   c. Why was the speaker so surprised to find her dead?
   d. What did 'she' have in her hand?

3. *'But when this lady hears that I am arriving, she is alarmed.'*
   a. Who said these words? Who was the 'lady' being spoken of?
   b. What information did the speaker reveal about the lady?
   c. Why was the lady alarmed and what did she do then?
   d. Did she succeed in her plan?

Life Skills and Values — festive traditions

1. What are the different Christmas traditions mentioned by the author? Give examples from the story to support your answer.
2. Does the ending of the story bring in joy and merriment as the occasion of Christmas should?
3. Do you think that traditions and rituals are an integral part of any festival, or should we do away with them? Explain your answer with examples.

Vocabulary

words related to celebrations

A. Find ten words related to celebrations in the word grid.

P	U	R	I	T	U	A	L	T	G	V	I	S	S	P
A	C	T	R	A	D	I	T	I	O	N	N	R	V	R
R	C	L	H	Z	B	B	R	F	E	A	S	T	Y	E
T	E	S	F	X	S	C	O	S	T	U	M	E	K	S
Y	R	U	S	M	G	B	E	F	E	O	L	D	J	E
Y	E	B	I	R	T	H	D	A	Y	N	Q	R	C	N
E	M	N	K	E	V	P	L	R	D	H	Q	H	G	T
C	O	B	L	W	G	A	T	H	E	R	I	N	G	S
F	N	B	A	N	Q	U	E	T	K	A	X	N	L	P
A	Y	G	J	A	Z	R	Q	Q	R	W	X	D	T	M

verbs with similar meaning

Read these sentences.

'Emily!' he **roared**. 'Why do you let the cook put glass in the puddings?'
'Glass?' **cried** Miss Endicott, astonished.
'Mr Poirot! Do wake up! Something dreadful has happened!' **screamed** Johnnie.

The highlighted verbs in these sentences have similar meanings.

B. **Classify the verbs according to the base verb they share their meanings with and write them in the correct columns.**

sense	murmur	listen	experience	observe
heed	notice	chat	glance	believe
catch	utter	understand	whisper	spot
attend	say	think	look	hark

speak	see	hear	feel

Grammar

tenses: perfect and perfect continuous

The **present perfect tense** is used to talk about an action completed in the recent past but whose effects still remain.

Example: Something dreadful **has happened**.

The **present perfect continuous tense** is used to talk about an action that started in the past but is still going on at the time of speaking.

Example: You **have been spoofing** us all the time.

The **past perfect tense** is used to talk about a past action that was completed before another past action began.

Example: The pudding **had been made** three days ago.

The **past perfect continuous tense** is used to talk about an action that took place in the past and continued for a period of time before it was completed.

Example: Nancy **had been lying** in the snow for quite some time.

The **future perfect tense** is used to talk about a future activity that will be finished by or before a specific time in the future.

Example: By tomorrow, Mr Levering and his sister **will have escaped**.

The **future perfect continuous tense** is used to talk about an ongoing activity which has not yet been completed but will be at a specified time in the future.

Example: By this time next year, the museum **will have been displaying** the ruby for two years.

A. Complete the sentences using the correct form of the given verbs.

1. The parrot _________________ (learn) several new words today.
2. Jake was hospitalized because he _________________ (break) his leg.
3. She _________________ (try) to solve the crossword for half an hour.
4. Tulika _________________ (stay) in this city for five years when her father got transferred.
5. Ravi _________________ (just enter) the hall when the film began.
6. I _________________ (clean) my room for an hour when it strikes nine.
7. I _________________ (climb) this mountain for over two hours now.
8. The old lady _________________ (feed) her dog by noon.

auxiliary verbs

You have learned that verbs denote action. They are of two kinds: main verbs and auxiliary verbs.

Auxiliary verbs or **helping verbs** are used with the main verbs to complete their meaning. The **primary auxiliary verbs** are *be (is, am, are, was, were), do (do, does, did)*, and *have (have, has, had)*.

Modal auxiliaries or **modals** are helping verbs that give additional information about the function of the main verbs that follow them. They indicate likelihood, ability, capability, willingness, possibility, permission and obligation. The modal auxiliaries are *can, could, may, might, must, shall, should, will* and *would*.

Examples: Nancy's hand **had** gone stiff and cold. (primary auxiliary)
We **can** use red paint.
I **could** frighten him with it.
You **must** send for the police.
} modal auxiliaries

B. Fill in the blanks with suitable primary and modal auxiliary verbs.

1. We _____________ look both ways before crossing a street.
2. Cinderella _____________ changed into a princess by the fairy godmother.
3. I _____________ type much faster before.
4. I _____________ reading this interesting book on dolphins now.
5. He _____________ worked on this science project very hard.
6. I _____________ knit a sweater for my sister for her birthday.
7. You _____________ use the swimming pool till 7 p.m.
8. You _____________ let me know before you leave.

Study Skills

Dictionary Skills

words of French origin

Look at these words from the story.

curious **disagree** **trifle** **haste**

These are English words which have their origins in the French language.

Use a dictionary to find the meanings of these words of French origin.

1. chef
2. petite
3. faux
4. ballad
5. en route
6. couture
7. caramel
8. regime

Listening

listening for facts

Listen to a passage on the celebration of Basanta Utsav and write whether these statements are true (T) or false (F). Correct the false statements.

1. The name *Visva Bharati* highlights the communion of the world with India. ☐
2. *Basanta Utsav* takes place in autumn. ☐
3. *Aamro Kunjo* is a garden of mangrove plants. ☐
4. Women are adorned with *palash* flowers. ☐
5. Tagore compared the flowers with bright red rubies. ☐
6. People hold colours in baskets woven with ribbons. ☐
7. They dance to the tunes of Rabindra Sangeet. ☐

Dictation

You will now listen to a short passage on fish and chips and write it down. Each sentence will be repeated twice. Listen carefully and be careful not to make any spelling errors.

Speaking

enacting the story as a play

Work in groups and enact the story as a play, following these steps.

1. Divide the events of the story into three scenes.
2. Make a list of the characters and assign roles. Choose someone to be the narrator, to hold the events of the play together.
3. Use lines from the story to prepare dialogues for the characters.
4. Use the front of the classroom as a makeshift stage with ordinary objects doubling up as props.

Writing

notice writing

A. A notice is a formal written communication to inform a group of people about an event. It is short and contains only the essential details of the event. Imagine that you are the organizer of the theatre club in your school. The club plans to put up a play based on the story *The Theft of the Ruby*. Write a notice inviting interested students to audition for the play. Mention the details of the play, and the date, time and venue for the audition.

invitation

An invitation is a message written to invite somebody to an event. Look at this sample invitation.

Dear Rehana,
We are celebrating our daughter's first birthday at Udayan Banquet Hall, on 25 June, and would love to have you and your family join us.
We cordially invite you to the party at 6 p.m.

Yours sincerely,
Rohith and Seema
R.S.V.P.
Rohith Moravineni
9830176009

B. Write a message to your friend, inviting him/her to the Christmas party at your house. Mention that the movie *A Christmas Carol* will be screened, and that Santa Claus will be paying a visit.

Now I can... — Self-Assessment

- read and enjoy a thrilling mystery.
- identify words related to celebrations and classify verbs with similar meaning.
- understand and use the perfect and perfect continuous tenses, and use auxiliary verbs.
- research words of French origin, and enact the story as a play.
- write a notice and an invitation.

Read at Leisure

A Christmas Carol: This book by Charles Dickens is about Ebenezer Scrooge, a mean and miserable old man with no friends, who is visited by three ghosts one cold Christmas Eve.

The Adventure of the Blue Carbuncle: This story by Arthur Conan Doyle accounts how Sherlock Holmes, the celebrated detective, solves the mystery of a priceless gem turning up inside a Christmas goose abandoned on a London street.

14 I Wave Good-bye When Butter Flies

Jack Prelutsky

Reading

Have you ever looked at certain words and thought about how they might have been coined? Read this fun poem to find out how everyday things take on extraordinary qualities.

I wave good-bye when butter flies[1]
and cheer a boxing match,
I've often watched my pillow fight[2],
I've sewn a cabbage patch,
I like to dance at basket balls
or lead a rubber band,
I've **marvelled** at a **spelling bee**,
I've helped a peanut stand.

It's possible a pencil points[3],
but does a **lemon drop**?
Does coffee break or **chocolate kiss**,
and will a soda pop?
I share my milk with drinking straws,
my meals with chewing gum,
and should I see my pocket change,
I'll hear my kettle drum.

It makes me sad when lettuce leaves,
I laugh when **dinner rolls**,
I wonder if the kitchen sinks
and if a salad bowls,
I've listened to a diamond ring,
I've waved a football fan,
and if a chimney sweeps the floor,
I'm sure the garbage can.

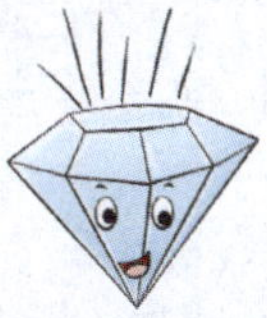

Literary terms

1. This is an example of a **pun**. The poet makes a pun on the word 'butterflies'. It has two meanings here: 1. colourful flying insects, 2. the act of butter flying in the air.
2. This is an example of **personification**. The pillow has been imagined as a person who is having a fight. This device too has been used by the poet frequently in this poem.
3. This is an example of **alliteration**, as the 'p' sound is repeated in consecutive words.

Food for thought

In America, a fizzy drink is called a *soda pop*. The same items have different British and American names. *Fries* are called *chips* in American English, whereas *chips* in American English are called *crisps* in British English.

marvelled: to be impressed by something
spelling bee: a competition in which people have to spell difficult words
lemon drop: a small, hard, lemon-flavoured candy
chocolate kiss: a type of chocolate candy
dinner rolls: small round pieces of bread provided with a meal

About the poet

Jack Prelutsky (born 1940) is an American writer of children's poetry. He has published over fifty poetry collections, including *Nightmares: Poems to Trouble Your Sleep*, and *Behold the Bold Umbrellaphant and Other Poems*. His works have been translated into many languages.

Food for thought

A kettle drum is a large drum, shaped like a bowl. It is a musical instrument that apparently originated in the Middle East. They are usually played in pairs, referred to as the *timpani*, with the two drums tuned to different pitches.

Understanding the poem

A. Complete these lines from the poem.

1. I wave goodbye when butter ______________ (melts/flies) and cheer a ______________ (boxing/wrestling) match.
2. I like to ______________ (skip/dance) at basket balls and lead ______________ (an elastic/a rubber) band.
3. Does coffee ______________ (break/spill) or ______________ (candy/chocolate) kiss?
4. It makes me sad when ______________ (cabbage/lettuce) leaves... I ______________ (cry/laugh) when dinner rolls.
5. I've listened to a ______________ (ruby/diamond) ring... I've waved a ______________ (basketball/football) fan.
6. If a chimney ______________ (sweeps/mops) the floor, I'm sure the garbage ______________ (can/bag).

B. Answer the questions with reference to context.

1. *I've marvelled at a spelling bee,*
   I've helped a peanut stand.
   a. Why has the poet marvelled at a 'spelling bee'?
   b. What is an actual spelling bee?
   c. Explain the pun used in the second line.
2. *I share my milk with drinking straws,*
   my meals with chewing gum,
   and should I see my pocket change,
   I'll hear my kettle drum.
   a. What are the everyday things the poet talks about in the quoted lines?
   b. Explain the pun used in the last two lines.
   c. What is the other literary device that the poet has used in these lines?

Life Skills and Values humour, appreciating everyday things

1. Did you find the poem funny? Give two examples and state why they make you laugh.
2. How does the poet use wordplay to create funny visuals for us? Do you think the poem helps us look at ordinary things in a new light?

Vocabulary

homophones

Look at these words.

bee (a black and yellow flying insect that can sting)

be (to exist)

break (damage or separate into parts)

brake (a device for slowing or stopping a vehicle)

These words are homophones.

Homophones are words that have the same pronunciation but different spellings and meanings.

A. Replace the underlined words with correct homophones to make meaningful sentences.

1. He placed the flours inside the glass vase.
2. She will right a letter to her sister tomorrow.
3. Witch book do you want to borrow this week?
4. Her father has taught her to tie different sailor's nots.
5. My mother pored me a glass of cold lemonade.
6. This dress is too lose, and does not fit me at all.
7. We could catch a glimpse of the see right from our hotel balcony.
8. My dog stairs at me greedily whenever I open a packet of chips.

pun

A **pun** is a form of word play that uses multiple meanings of a term, or similar-sounding words, to create a humorous effect.

Example: In the line 'I've listened to a diamond ring', the poet makes a pun on the word 'ring'. It has two meanings here:
1. an item of jewellery worn on the finger,
2. the sound of a telephone or a bell.

B. Identify the puns in the sentences and write their meanings.

1. It's pointless to write with a broken nib.

   Meanings: 1. without a pointed tip

   2. without meaning
2. Her uncle is a baker for he kneads money.
3. His cycle can't stand on its own because it is two-tired.
4. Jane is a good doctor; she doesn't lose patients.
5. 'Mine is a long and sad tale,' said the mouse.
6. A horse is quite a stable animal.
7. He has been to the dentist many times so he knows the drill by now.

Activity

advertisement

An advertisement is created for the promotion of a product or service or even an event. Create an advertisement for butter and cheese, in the form of a presentation. It should have the following points:

- an imaginary brand name
- a short and crisp description
- nutritional information
- a tag line (This is a phrase that comes at the beginning or the end, and is meant to be amusing or easy to remember).

Now I can... **Self-Assessment**

- o read and enjoy a humorous poem full of puns.
- o use homophones and identify puns.
- o create an advertisement in the form of a presentation.

Read at Leisure

The ABC: This poem by Spike Milligan describes a funny conversation among the alphabets who come alive and talk of various language rules.

A Flea And A Fly In A Flue: This short poem by Ogden Nash uses wordplay and alliteration to tell the story of a fly and a flea.

Answers to Take Off:

A. 1. Diwali 2. Holi 3. Dusshera 4. Eid 5. Easter 6. Onam 7. Rakhi 8. Lohri

B. 1. Waldorf salad 2. Bombay duck 3. Chicken Chettinad 4. Bourbon biscuit 5. French toast 6. Turkish delight 7. Malabar paratha 8. Black Forest cake

VIII

Tales of War

Take Off

A. Find the antonyms of the given words related to war in the grid and circle them.

1. retreat
2. peace
3. cowardice
4. defend
5. free
6. defeat

E	O	V	X	C	M	E	M	A	A	L	Y	F	J	P
X	D	D	R	S	V	E	Z	C	A	P	T	I	V	E
C	N	H	A	U	B	K	E	Q	J	H	P	C	Y	P
D	J	Q	J	Y	V	F	E	S	A	T	Y	K	P	R
R	K	M	G	O	I	O	P	S	D	O	R	F	W	X
I	P	M	A	G	C	B	R	A	V	E	R	Y	J	F
U	V	M	L	A	T	P	M	S	A	T	T	A	C	K
G	P	O	X	A	O	V	V	P	N	I	P	X	F	E
Y	O	M	K	L	R	W	A	R	C	P	K	X	Z	J
S	T	D	V	P	Y	Z	G	R	E	P	C	O	N	X

B. Fill in the blanks with the correct form of the verbs to learn about the Battle of Blenheim, which you will read about in this unit.

capture   launch   drown   situate   form   suffer

The Battle of Blenheim was fought in 1704. It took place in the town of Blenheim, ____________ near the Danube River, in Bavaria. The French and Bavarian armies ____________ one of the sides, and their opponents were England and her allies. The English soldiers ____________ a successful attack against the French, driving them into the river. As a result, the French ____________ defeat with huge losses. The Allies ____________ 13,000 Franco-Bavarian troops while approximately 18,000 more ____________ in the river.

15 The Christmas Truce

Aaron Shepard

Reading

War can often put people who would have been friends on opposite sides. Read this play in which English and German soldiers, guarding the trenches on opposite sides of the border, set their differences aside for one special occasion. The play is imagined in the form of letters being read out by four English soldiers who are in the trenches.

Characters

Soldier 1 **Soldier 3**

Soldier 2 **Soldier 4**

Food for thought

World War I began in 1914 with the assassination of Archduke Franz Ferdinand of Austria-Este in Sarajevo. It was fought between Germany, Austria-Hungary, Bulgaria and the Ottoman Empire who formed the Central powers, and Great Britain, France, Russia, Japan, Italy, Romania and the United States who formed the Allied powers. Advanced military technologies and trench warfare caused destruction of life on a scale never seen before. The war ended in 1918, with the victory of the Allied powers.

Soldier 1 *(to audience)*: Christmas Day, 1914. Dear mother,

Soldier 2 *(to audience)*: My darling Meg,

Soldier 3 *(to audience)*: My good friend Charles,

Soldier 4 *(to audience)*: My dear sister Janet,

Soldier 1: It is 2:00 in the morning and most of our men are asleep in their **dugouts**.

Soldier 2: Yet I could not sleep myself before writing to you of the wonderful events of Christmas Eve.

Soldier 3: In truth, what happened seems almost like a fairy tale, and if I hadn't been through it myself, I would **scarce** believe it.

Soldier 4: Just imagine: While you and the family sang carols before the fire there in London, I did the same with enemy soldiers here on the battlefields of France!

Soldier 1: As I wrote before, there has been little serious fighting of late. The first battles of the war left so many dead that both sides have held back until replacements could come from home. So, we have mostly stayed in our **trenches** and waited.

Where were the soldiers waiting and for what?

Soldier 2: But what a terrible waiting it has been! Knowing that any moment an **artillery** shell might land and explode beside us in

truce: an agreement to stop fighting, usually temporarily

dugouts: rough shelters used by soldiers, made by digging into the ground

scarce: hardly

trenches: long deep holes dug in the ground in which soldiers can be protected from enemy attacks

artillery: large, heavy guns which are often moved on wheels the trench, killing or **maiming** several men. And in daylight not daring to lift our heads above ground, for fear of a **sniper's** bullet.

Soldier 3: And the rain—it has fallen almost daily. Of course, it collects right in our trenches, where we must **bail** it **out** with pots and pans. And with the rain has come mud—a good foot or more deep.

Soldier 4: It splatters and **cakes** everything, and constantly sucks at our boots. One new **recruit** got his feet stuck in it, and then his hands too when he tried to get out—just like in that American story of the tar baby!

Soldier 1: Through all this, we couldn't help feeling curious about the German soldiers across the way. After all, they faced the same dangers we did, and **slogged** about in the same muck.

Soldier 2: What's more, their first trench was only fifty yards from ours. Between us lay **no-man's-land**, bordered on both sides by barbed wire—yet they were close enough that we sometimes heard their voices.

Soldier 3: Of course, we hated them whenever they killed our friends. But other times, we joked about them and almost felt we had something in common.

Soldier 4: And now it seems they felt the same.

Soldier 1: Just yesterday morning—Christmas Eve Day—we had our first good freeze. Cold as we were, we welcomed it, because at least the mud froze solid.

Soldier 2: Everything was **tinged** white with frost, while a bright sun shone over all. Perfect Christmas weather.

Soldier 3: During the day, there was little **shelling** or rifle fire from either side. And as darkness fell on our Christmas Eve, the shooting stopped entirely.

Soldier 4: Our first complete silence in months! We hoped it might promise a peaceful holiday, but we didn't count on it. We'd been told the Germans might attack and try to catch us off guard.

Food for thought

The tar baby features in Joel Chandler Harris' *Uncle Remus* stories. It is the story of a doll made of tar and turpentine. It was used by Br'er Fox to try to trap Br'er Rabbit. But the cunning rabbit was able to outsmart the fox and escape his trap.

maiming: causing severe injury like the loss of a limb
sniper: a shooter who shoots from a hidden position
bail out: scoop out water
cakes: covers something with a thick layer that becomes hard when it dries
recruit: a new member of the armed forces
slogged: worked hard and steadily at something
no-man's-land: an area between enemy forces over which no control has been established
tinged: coloured lightly
shelling: dropping of bombs

Soldier 1: I went to the dugout to rest, and lying on my cot, I must have drifted asleep. All at once my friend was shaking me awake, saying, 'Come and see! See what the Germans are doing!' I grabbed my rifle, stumbled out into the trench, and stuck my head cautiously above the sandbags.

Soldier 2: I never hope to see a stranger and more lovely sight. **Clusters** of tiny lights were shining all along the German line, left and right as far as the eye could see.

Soldier 3: 'What is it?' I asked in **bewilderment**, and someone answered, 'Christmas trees!'

Soldier 4: And so it was. The Germans had placed Christmas trees in front of their trenches, lit by candle or lantern like **beacons** of good will.

Soldier 1: And then we heard their voices raised in song.
(singing) 'Stille nacht, heilige nacht…'

Soldier 2: This carol may not yet be familiar to us in Britain, but one soldier knew it and translated: 'Silent night, holy night.' I've never heard one lovelier—or more meaningful, in that quiet, clear night, its dark softened by a first-quarter moon.

What did the German carol translate to?

Soldier 3: When the song finished, the men in our trenches **applauded**. Yes, British soldiers applauding Germans!

Soldier 4: Then one of our own men started singing, and we all joined in.
(singing) 'The first Noel, the angel did say…'

Soldier 1: In truth, we sounded not nearly as good as the Germans, with their fine **harmonies**. But they responded with enthusiastic applause of their own and then began another. *(singing)* 'O Tannenbaum, o Tannenbaum…'

Soldier 2: Then we replied.
(singing) 'O come all ye faithful…'

Soldier 3: But this time they joined in, singing the words in Latin. *(singing)* 'Adeste fideles…'

Soldier 4: British and German **harmonizing** across no-man's-land! I would have thought nothing could be more amazing—but what came next was more so.

Soldier 1: 'English, come over!' we heard one of them shout. 'You no shoot, we no shoot.'

Soldier 2: There in the trenches, we looked at each other in bewilderment. Then one of us shouted jokingly, 'You come over here.'

---

clusters: groups
bewilderment: confusion
beacons: guiding lights
applauded: clapped

harmonies: the pleasant combination of different musical notes at the same time
harmonizing: singing in agreement with different pitches of voice

Soldier 3: To our **astonishment**, we saw two figures rise from the trench, climb over their barbed wire, and **advance** unprotected across no-man's-land.

Soldier 4: One of them called, 'Send officer to talk.'

Soldier 1: I saw one of our men lift his rifle at the ready[1], and no doubt others did the same—but our captain called out, 'Hold your fire[2].' Then he climbed out and went to meet the Germans halfway.

Soldier 2: We heard them talking, and a few minutes later, the captain came back with a German glove in his hand! 'We've agreed there will be no shooting before midnight tomorrow,' he announced. 'But sentries are to remain on duty, and the rest of you, stay alert.'

Common idioms and proverbs

1. **at the ready:** This idiom means that something is available to be used immediately.
2. **hold your fire:** This idiom means to wait, and be calm. Here, it means to refrain from firing literally.

Soldier 3: Across the way, we could make out groups of two or three men starting out of trenches and coming toward us.

Soldier 4: Then some of us were climbing out too, and in minutes more, there we were in no-man's-land, over a hundred soldiers and officers of each side, shaking hands with men we'd been trying to kill just hours earlier!

Soldier 1: Before long a **bonfire** was built, and around it we mingled—British khaki and German grey. I must say, the Germans were the better dressed, with fresh uniforms for the holiday.

Soldier 2: Only a couple of our men knew German, but more of the Germans knew English. I asked one of them why that was.

'Because many have worked in England!' he said. 'Before all this, I was a waiter at the Hotel Cecil. Perhaps I waited on your table!'

'Perhaps you did!' I said, laughing.

Why were the Germans better dressed?

Soldier 3: One German told me he had a **fiancée** in London and that the war had interrupted their plans for marriage. I said, 'Don't worry. We'll have you beat by Easter, then you can come back and marry her.'

He laughed at that. Then he asked if I'd send her a postcard he'd give me later, and I promised I would.

Food for thought

German soldiers in the nineteenth and twentieth centuries wore a spiked helmet known as the Pickelhaube or the Pickelhelm.

Soldier 4: Another German had been a porter at Victoria Station. He showed me a picture of his family back in Munich. I told him I should like to meet them someday. He beamed and said he would like that very much and gave me his family's address.

Soldier 1: Even those who could not converse could still exchange gifts—our mufflers for their gloves, our tea for their coffee, English food for German food. Badges and buttons from uniforms changed owners, and one of our lads walked off with the **infamous** spiked helmet!

advance: (here) move forward
fiancée: a woman engaged to be married
infamous: notorious

Soldier 2: I myself traded a **jackknife** for a leather equipment belt—a fine **souvenir** to show when I get home.

What did Soldier 2 get in return for his jackknife?

Soldier 3: Newspapers too changed hands, and the Germans howled with laughter at ours. They assured us that France was finished and Russia nearly beaten too.

Soldier 4: We told them that was nonsense, and one of them said, 'Well, you believe your newspapers and we'll believe ours.'

Soldier 1: Clearly they are lied to—yet after meeting these men, I wonder how truthful our own newspapers have been.

Soldier 2: These are not the 'savage **barbarians**' we've read so much about. They are men with homes and families, hopes and fears, principles and, yes, love of country.

Soldier 3: In other words, men like ourselves.

Soldier 1: As it grew late, a few more songs were traded around the fire, and then all joined in for—I am not lying to you— 'Auld Lang Syne.'

Soldier 2: Then we parted with promises to meet again tomorrow,

Soldier 3: And even some talk of a football match.

Soldier 4: I was just starting back to the trenches when an older German clutched my arm. 'My God,' he said, 'why cannot we have peace and all go home?' I told him gently, 'That you must ask your emperor.' He looked at me then, **searchingly**. 'Perhaps, my friend. But also, we must ask our hearts.'

jackknife: a large knife with a folding blade

souvenir: an object that recalls a certain place, occasion, or person

barbarians: people who behave in an uncivilized or cruel manner

searchingly: closely

Comprehension

A. Answer the questions.

1. What were the four soldiers doing at the start of the play? Who were they writing to?
2. Why were the British soldiers curious about the Germans?
3. List the songs sung by the soldiers of both the sides.
4. What instructions did the British captain give his men?
5. How did many of the Germans know English?

6. What were the gifts exchanged between the soldiers?
7. What was the older German soldier's wish?

B. Answer the questions with reference to context.

1. *'But what a terrible waiting it has been!'*
   a. Who said these words? What 'waiting' is being spoken about?
   b. What made the waiting terrible? How did the weather add to the problems?
   c. What incident resulted in the reference to the 'tar baby' story?
2. *'Come and see! See what the Germans are doing!'*
   a. Who said these words and to whom?
   b. What were the Germans doing and when?
   c. How did the English soldiers react?
   d. What arrangement was reached between the soldiers?
3. *'Don't worry. We'll have you beat by Easter, then you can come back and marry her.'*
   a. Who said these words and to whom?
   b. Why did the speaker say these words?
   c. What did the person spoken to want the speaker to do for him?
   d. Describe a similar encounter that Soldier 4 had immediately after this.

Life Skills and Values — brotherhood, humanity

1. What lesson did you learn from the play? What do you think the old German soldier meant when he said that the answer lay in 'our hearts'?
2. How is this play relevant in today's world? Give examples to support your answer.

Vocabulary

contextual usage

A. Fill in the blanks with these words from the story.

frost   exchange   curious   advance   beaten   scarce   souvenirs   tinged

1. The ______________ boy hid in the shadows and listened to the adults talking.
2. The temperature dipped last night, and the windows were covered in ______________.
3. The brave general ordered an ______________ on the enemy lines.
4. Every year, ______________ students from Europe attend classes with us.

5. The victorious team was consoling the players of the team they had ________________.
6. The sunset sky, ________________ golden, made for a mesmerizing scene.
7. As the siege went on, food became increasingly ________________ inside the fort.
8. It was an empty stretch of the beach, with only a tiny shop selling ________________.

idioms related to the army

B. Match these idioms related to the army with their meanings.

Idioms	Meanings
1. bite the bullet	a. very quickly, immediately
2. take flak	b. back away or go away quickly
3. on the double	c. (of a group) work closely together and defend themselves
4. watch your back	d. start to deal with a difficult situation
5. close ranks	e. receive a lot of negative feedback
6. in the trenches	f. be careful
7. beat a hasty retreat	g. place or situation in which people do very difficult work

C. Fill in the blanks with the idioms from the previous exercise. You may have to make some changes.

1. He's ________________ a lot of ________________ for his reckless decisions.
2. Nurse, I need a copy of the patient's report ________________.
3. The officers would always ________ around their own, and try to justify their actions.
4. As soon as the pickpocket realised that he had been noticed, he tried to ________.
5. Pritha decided to ________________ and own up to the mischief.
6. The volunteers are working daily ______________________ to improve the living conditions of the poor.
7. The bowler better ________________. He has been warned twice by the umpire.

Grammar

types of sentences

You know that sentences are of four types.

An **assertive sentence** states something or provides some information. It can be positive or negative.

Example: It is 2:00 in the morning and most of our men are asleep in their dugouts.

An **interrogative sentence** asks a question. It can be a *wh-* question or a *yes/no* question.

Example: Why cannot we have peace and all go home?

An **imperative sentence** gives a command, an instruction, a piece of advice, or makes a request.

Example: You come over here.

An **exclamatory sentence** expresses strong emotions or feelings of excitement, joy, surprise, anger or sadness.

Example: One of our lads walked off with the infamous spiked helmet!

A. Identify the types of sentences and write (A) for assertive, (I) for interrogative, (E) for exclamatory and (IM) for imperative.

1. Hurrah, our summer vacation begins today! ☐
2. Maya is a trained Kathak dancer. ☐
3. Do you think Hailey knows where we are going? ☐
4. Do not walk on the grass. ☐
5. I don't like sandwiches at all. ☐
6. Don't you think the film was quite funny? ☐
7. Alas, India lost the final match to Australia! ☐
8. Please pass the salt and pepper. ☐

Assertive sentences can be changed to interrogative and exclamatory sentences and vice versa.
Look at the table to understand how one type of sentence can be written as another.

Assertive	Interrogative	Exclamatory
It has been a terrible waiting.	Has it been a terrible waiting?	What a terrible waiting it has been!
We cannot have peace and all go home.	Why cannot we have peace and all go home?	Alas! We cannot have peace and all go home.

B. Rewrite the sentences as instructed.

1. Why should we waste time here? (change to assertive)
2. This is not the way to behave with your elders. (change to interrogative)

3. How charming you look in this hat! (change to assertive)
4. There is no way of winning the match. (change to interrogative)
5. This is quite a silly excuse. (change to exclamatory)
6. It is very hot in Delhi. (change to exclamatory)
7. Have they lost the battle? (change to assertive)
8. The mountains look so majestic. (change to exclamatory)

conditional sentences using *if* and *unless*

Read these sentences.
If I hadn't been through it myself, I would scarce believe it.
Unless the emperor agrees, you cannot stop this war.

In both the sentences, the condition in the second part is not fulfilled until the action in the first part is complete. These are conditional sentences.

When we use *unless* to write conditional sentences, we use *not*.

C. Rewrite the sentences according to the given instructions.

1. Unless you stop talking, you will not be able to pay attention. (Begin: If you stop...)
2. If you are free in the evening, we could go watch a movie. (Begin: Unless you are...)
3. Unless you drive fast, we will not be able to reach on time. (Begin: If you drive...)
4. If they do not rehearse now, they will not be ready for the concert. (Begin: Unless they rehearse...)
5. Unless she pays the rent on time, she will not be able to stay here. (Begin: If she pays...)
6. Do not try that technique unless you are sure about it. (Begin: If you are sure...)
7. Unless the rain stops, we won't be able to play outside. (Begin: If the rain...)

Study Skills

Pronunciation

words with silent consonants

Read these words aloud.
knapsack   **w**rath   lis**t**en   Chris**t**mas   **h**onour
You will notice that the highlighted consonants are silent when the words are pronounced.

Read the list of words aloud and circle the silent consonant.

1. doubt
2. half
3. knee
4. wrong
5. ballet
6. gnome
7. honesty
8. yacht

Listening

listening for details

Listen to a passage on Florence Nightingale and fill in the blanks.

1. Florence was born into a wealthy ______________ family.
2. She always showed a keen interest in ______________ and caring for those ______________ than herself.
3. In those days nursing was considered a profession fit for the ______________.
4. During the ______________, she and her fellow nurses reached the barracks in ______________.
5. Wounded soldiers were dying from ______________ rather than ______________.
6. Florence and her team started ______________ the hospital.
7. Florence would walk at night with a ______________, and the soldiers would call her ______________.

Speaking

narrating a chain story

A chain story is one in which each section or line is written by a different person, picking up from where the previous one left off. Work in groups and narrate a chain story on the topic 'a Christmas gift to remember', with each student saying one line of the story. Remember that you have to link your sentence to the context of what has happened previously, and at the same time, be imaginative while adding new details. You can talk about the following points:

- the surprise of an unexpected gift
- something that you had been secretly hoping for; something strange and funny
- feeling of thankfulness/mystery surrounding the giver of the gift
- revelation and resolution; Christmas cheer all around

Writing

diary entry

Imagine that you are a soldier stationed in the German trenches, who has just returned after spending Christmas with the English soldiers. Write a diary entry about the events that took place in the no-man's-land on the Christmas of 1914.
You may use these points:

- how you and your fellow soldiers put out Christmas trees and sang carols
- the heart-warming reaction of the English soldiers
- how Christmas brought people close, erasing all borders
- your longing that the war would end soon and you could return home

Now I can... **Self-Assessment**

- read and understand a play on how war affects everybody in the same way, irrespective of nationality.
- use words in context, and idioms related to the army.
- understand and identify the different types of sentences, and use conditional sentences.
- pronounce words with silent consonants correctly.
- narrate a chain story, and write a diary entry.

Read at Leisure

The Boy in the Striped Pyjamas: This book by John Boyne is about the friendship between two children in a Nazi concentration camp during World War II.

Black Dove, White Raven: This book by Elizabeth Wein is a story of survival set in war-torn Ethiopia, about two children who pretend to be superheroes, saving each other from imaginary dangers.

narrative poem

16 After Blenheim

Robert Southey

Reading

Have you listened to stories from your elders about their lives and times? Read this poem about an old man narrating the story of a war to his two grandchildren.

It was a summer evening,
  Old Kaspar's work was done,
And he before his cottage door
  Was sitting in the sun,
And by him **sported** on the **green**
  His little grandchild Wilhelmine.

She saw her brother Peterkin
  Roll something large and round,
Which he beside the **rivulet**
  In playing there had found;
He came to ask what he had found,
  That was so large, and smooth, and round.

Old Kaspar took it from the boy,
  Who stood **expectant** by;
And then the old man shook his head,
  And, with a natural sigh,
''Tis some poor fellow's skull,' said he,
  'Who fell in the great victory.

'I find them in the garden,
  For there's many here about;
And often when I go to plough,
  The **ploughshare** turns them out!
For many thousand men,' said he,
  'Were **slain** in that great victory.'

Where was Kaspar sitting?

Food for thought

The Battle of Blenheim was the most famous victory for John Churchill, the first duke of Marlborough, and Prince Eugene of Savoy. In the battle, 12,000 men were killed or wounded on the British-allied side, while the opposition lost approximately 20,000 men.

sported: played
green: (here) a field covered with grass
rivulet: a small stream
expectant: waiting
ploughshare: the cutting blade of a plough
slain: killed

'Now tell us what 'twas all about,'
    Young Peterkin, he cries;
And little Wilhelmine looks up
    With wonder-waiting[1] eyes;
'Now tell us all about the war,
    And what they fought each other for.'

'It was the English,' Kaspar cried,
    'Who put the French to **rout**;
But what they fought each other for,
    I could not well make out;
But everybody said,' quoth he,
    'That 'twas a famous victory[2].

'My father lived at Blenheim then,
    Yon little stream **hard by**;
They burnt his dwelling to the ground,
    And he was forced to **fly**;
So with his wife and child he fled,
    Nor had he where to rest his head.

'With fire and sword the country round
    Was wasted far and wide...
... They say it was a shocking sight
    After the field was won;
But things like that, you know, must be
    After a famous victory.

'Great praise the Duke of Marlbro' won,
    And our good Prince Eugene.'
'Why, 'twas a very wicked thing!'
    Said little Wilhelmine.
'Nay... nay... my little girl,' quoth he,
    'It was a famous victory.

'And everybody praised the Duke
    Who this great fight did win.'
'But what good came of it at last?'
    Quoth little Peterkin.
'Why that I cannot tell,' said he,
    'But 'twas a famous victory.'

(abridged)

Literary terms

1. This is an example of **alliteration**, as the 'w' sound is repeated in consecutive words.
2. This is an instance of **repetition**. The line 'It was a famous victory' is repeated several times in the poem to stress that winning the battle was more important than the loss of lives it caused.

rout: an overwhelming defeat
yon: (archaic) that
hard by: quite near
fly: (here) run away, escape

About the poet

Robert Southey (1774–1843) was a biographer, poet, historian and scholar. He was a contemporary of the poets William Wordsworth and Samuel Taylor Coleridge, and one of his most famous contributions to literature is *The Story of the Three Bears*, the origin of the famous *Goldilocks* story. *The Inchcape Rock* and *Cataract of Lodore* are his other well-known poems.

Understanding the poem

A. Answer the questions in one word.

1. Who was Kaspar's grandson?
2. Which tool turned up skulls in the garden?
3. Who fought the French in the battle?
4. What was beside Kaspar's father's dwelling?
5. Name the prince Kaspar mentions in the poem.
6. Who won the battle?

B. Answer the questions with reference to context.

1. *...Old Kaspar's work was done...*
   a. Which time of the year was it?
   b. Who was Kaspar and what was he doing?
   c. Who was beside him and what was she doing?

2. *'They burnt his dwelling to the ground,/And he was forced to fly;'*
   a. Who said these words and to whom?
   b. Who was 'he'? Why was he 'forced to fly' and with whom?
   c. What was the effect of the battle on the countryside and the people?

3. *'...They say it was a shocking sight'*
   After the field was won...
   a. What is meant by the 'field'? What had happened to the 'country round'?
   b. What was Kaspar's reasoning for the devastation?
   c. Did his grandchildren agree with him? How did they react?

Life Skills and Values — effects of war

1. The poet repeats the lines 'twas a famous victory'. Do you think he really believed that the victory was something to be celebrated?
2. Do you think wars are necessary? Give reasons for your answer.

Vocabulary

rhyming couplets

Read these lines.

By him sported on the **green**
His little grandchild **Wilhelmine**.

In this pair of sentences, the ending words *green* and *Wilhelmine* rhyme. The thought or information given in the first line is completed in the second line, making these lines a **rhyming couplet**.

A. Identify three other rhyming couplets from the poem and underline the rhyming words.

repetition

Repetition is a literary device where the same word, phrase or a sentence is repeated at intervals to emphasize a particular idea, and also to create rhythm.
Example: In this poem, the line **It was a famous victory** is repeated several times.

B. Read these verses and identify the instances of repetition.

1. It was many and many a year ago,
   In a kingdom by the sea,
   That a maiden there lived whom you may know...
   I was a child and she was a child,
   In this kingdom by the sea...
2. O Captain! my Captain! our fearful trip is done,
   The ship has weather'd every rack, the prize we sought is won,
   The port is near, the bells I hear, the people all exulting
   While follow eyes the steady keel, the vessel grim and daring...
   ...O Captain! my Captain! rise up and hear the bells...
3. The woods are lovely, dark, and deep,
   But I have promises to keep
   And miles to go before I sleep,
   And miles to go before I sleep.

Activity

making a presentation

Work in pairs and find out about World War I. Make a slide show presentation to highlight the information you have collected.
You can include these points in your presentation.

- what sparked the war
- the duration of the war
- the countries that fought on both sides
- the outcome
- your views on war being a solution to international problems

Now I can... | **Self-Assessment**

- o read and understand a poem on the futility of a destructive war.
- o identify rhyming couplets and instances of repetition.
- o research and make a presentation on World War I.

Read at Leisure

The Charge of the Light Brigade: This poem by Alfred Lord Tennyson describes the courage of a brigade of 600 soldiers who rode into battle on horseback.

The Inchcape Rock: This poem by Robert Southey tells the story of a bell installed on a dangerous reef to warn travellers, and the fate suffered by the pirate who removed it.

IX

Overcoming Odds

Take Off

A. The Olympic Games is considered the world's biggest sports competition. Look at the Olympic symbol carefully and find the answers to these questions.

1. The Olympic symbol was designed by ______________.
2. The colours stand for those found in the ______________ of different countries.
3. The five rings symbolise the five different ______________.
4. The modern Olympic Games started in ______________.
5. The Olympic flag was used for the first time at the __________ Olympic games.
6. Before each Olympic game, the Olympic torch is lit in ______________.
7. The motto of the Olympics is *Citius, Altius, Fortius,* meaning ______________.

B. One of the best ways to overcome odds in life is to be positive. Work in pairs and find eight words in the grid related to the odds we face in life and ways of overcoming them.

S	C	L	C	H	A	L	L	E	N	G	E	S	P	C
D	O	U	B	T	M	N	X	U	J	P	F	P	G	Z
E	U	N	Q	S	B	J	Y	Q	I	E	Y	F	C	M
S	R	R	J	H	K	O	R	N	H	E	N	C	N	X
V	A	G	D	T	P	Y	R	D	T	Z	U	P	Z	O
W	G	C	O	N	F	I	D	E	N	C	E	Q	W	I
H	E	S	I	T	A	T	I	O	N	W	K	J	I	X
X	Q	K	S	D	X	E	N	P	V	V	E	Y	F	Z
N	S	A	C	H	I	E	V	E	M	E	N	T	K	G
Z	P	O	P	T	I	M	I	S	M	X	T	C	K	Z

non-fiction

17 India's Shining Girls

Reading

The world of sport is full of stories of women who have overcome great odds to make a name for themselves. Read on to learn about three such sportswomen from India.

The 2016 Olympics held at Rio de Janeiro, Brazil was very special for India. As many as 54 female Indian athletes participated, the highest ever, many of whom rose above countless **hurdles** to make India proud. As many of them prepare for the 2020 Tokyo Olympics, we look at a few remarkable Indian sportswomen who are showing the way[1] to others who will come after them.

Common idioms and proverbs

1. **show the way:** This idiom means to do something first so that other people can follow.

Magnificent Mary

In November 2018, MC Mary Kom defeated Ukranian boxer Hanna Okhota at the tenth Women's World Boxing Championships, making her the most successful boxer in the history of the **tournament**. By then, 35-year-old Kom had been the World Amateur Boxing champion for a record six times and was the only woman Indian boxer to have won an Olympic medal.

In a country of cricket fans, Mary Kom is one of the few sportspersons who is a household name. At 5 feet 2 inches, she is much shorter than most boxers. But she makes up for it with speed, **aggression**, strength and determination.

For this Muhammad Ali fan, the challenges in life started early. Born into a poor family in rural Manipur to **tenant farmers**, she often helped her parents in the *jhum* fields. She shifted from athletics to boxing after watching the boys fight at a local gym.

Originally named 'Chungneijang' by her

Food for thought

Jhum cultivation is widely practised in the northeastern states of India like Arunachal Pradesh and Tripura. Land is cleared for crops by felling or burning trees and agricultural production takes place on the cleared land for a few years till the land loses its fertility.

hurdles: difficulties
tournament: a trial of skill in a game
aggression: an attacking attitude
tenant farmers: people who farm land owned by another person and pay rent in cash or in a share of the crops

grandmother, she adopted the name 'Mary Kom', as it was easy to use at competitions. Mary kept her interest in boxing a secret from her father, himself an ex-wrestler, as he was concerned that boxing might damage her face. He found out when her photo appeared in a newspaper after she won the state boxing championship in the year 2000. She was 17 years old then. It took him three years to be **convinced** that Kom could take up boxing as a career.

In 2008, she won a silver medal at the Asian Women's Boxing Championship, after a two-year break, silencing **naysayers** who had said that it would be impossible for her to return to boxing after marriage.

What did Mary win in 2008?

Her dreams came true in 2012 when she **clinched** a bronze at the London Olympics. She received a standing **ovation** as she left the hall.

Boxing in India is dominated by men, but Mary Kom has made it her own. She has founded the Mary Kom-SAI Boxing Academy in Imphal to train young boxers. Mother to three children, the Padma Shri and Padma Bhushan awardee also runs a female-only fight club to train girls in self-defence.

Food for thought

SAI or the Sports Authority of India was set up in 1984 by the Indian government with the goal of promoting sports and games in the country. Besides providing training, coaches and sports infrastructure, SAI is also responsible for recruiting and nurturing sportspersons all over the nation.

'Winning the 2012 bronze medal was magnificent, but I would love to win a gold medal in the 2020 Tokyo Olympics,' she says.

Taking a leap of faith

At the 2016 Olympics, a **pint-sized** gymnast from Agartala, Tripura attempted the Produnova vault on the Olympic stage, as the world watched wide-eyed. One of the most difficult moves in gymnastics, the Produnova involves a **handspring** onto the vault, followed by two-and-a-half **somersaults** off the **vault**. It can **catapult** a gymnast to the top of the competitors' list. Twenty-five-year-old Dipa Karmakar perfected it by practising it 'a 1000 times' over three months.

Brought up in a family of limited means, far away from the world of an elite sport like gymnastics, Dipa knew that to get noticed for the big league international competitions, she would have to take risks. 'My coach and I wanted to win a medal for India. We knew we had to do it anyhow and this vault was the answer,' she has said.

convinced: to feel completely sure
naysayers: people who habitually oppose something
clinched: secured
ovation: continued applause
pint sized: tiny, small in size
handspring: a gymnastic move which involves landing on one's hands without any other part of the body touching the base, starting from a standing pose
vault: (here) a padded block on legs, used in gymnastics
somersault: an acrobatic movement in which the body moves over completely in a circular motion either forwards or backwards in the air
catapult: (here) move quickly; leap

'I want to inspire the next generation so that in 10 to 15 years, India can send a full gymnastics team to the Olympics and not just one athlete,' Dipa said after she stood fourth in the Rio Olympics, missing the medal by just 0.15 points.

Dipa started training as a gymnast at the tender age of five, when her father enrolled her at the local gymnasium he himself had once attended. **Adversity** was a constant companion. She has flat feet, a disadvantage affecting her jumps and landings. She had little funding or **infrastructure**. The training grounds would sometimes get flooded. But the duo had creativity and the dream of making Dipa a world class gymnast. They built **makeshift** apparatus from a pile of **crash mats** and the **discarded** parts of a second-hand scooter.

Food for thought

The Produnova vault was named after the Russian gymnast Yelena Produnova. She was the first to complete the vault successfully in 1933. Due to its difficulty and chances of serious injury, the vault is sometimes referred to as 'the vault of death', and had been tried by only four gymnasts before.

At what age did Dipa start training?

In 2007, Dipa won the Junior National Championships for the first time. She has won 77 medals since then, including 67 golds.

After the Olympics, Dipa suffered a big **setback**. She had a serious **ligament** injury which put her out of the game for two years. But in 2018, she made a comeback[2] with a gold medal at the FIG Artistic Gymnastics World Challenge Cup in Turkey.

Dipa's goal is to bring a medal back for India at the 2020 Olympics, though she may not try the Produnova again.

The Dhing Express

For Hima Das, running has been **second nature**. She ran in anger, after a car was 'too full' to **accommodate** her on a ride to school. She ran from her mother the same day, having reached home with knees bruised as a result of the car chase. As an athlete, too, she has continued running with **steadfast** determination — in tracks across Assam, in coaching camps in Patiala and Sonepat, and even in those rare races where she 'wanted to give up midway'. This Arjuna awardee's never-say-die[3] attitude has taken her from the paddy fields of Dhing, a small village in Assam where she played football with boys, to the IAAF World Under-20 Championships in Tampere, Finland, where she won gold in July 2018. This was India's first gold at an international **track** event.

Common idioms and proverbs

2. **make a comeback:** This idiom means to achieve success after failure or an injury.
3. **never-say-die:** This idiom means to not give up.

It was in 2012 that Md Shamsul Hoque, a physical education teacher at the Navodaya Vidyalaya in Nagaon, Assam, had noticed

adversity: unfavourable circumstances
infrastructure: facilities and systems
makeshift: temporary substitute
crash mats: foam pads used for protection while performing stunts
discarded: cast or thrown away
setback: something that reverses progress
ligament: a tissue band holding bones together
second nature: something that one does quite easily, because it is part of their character or they have done it so many times
accommodate: provide room, seat
steadfast: firm in purpose
track: a piece of ground with a special surface for people to have races on

the girl at an inter-school camp. She always reached before practice and won all the races. Impressed, Hoque informed the Nagaon Sports Association about Hima. His **intervention** got Hima, who had been playing football in local tournaments, into athletics.

When Hima shifted to Guwahati to train in 2017, she had little money, no running **spikes** and lived in a small room with a leaky roof. 'She was supremely dedicated. No matter what she went through the night before, she would be at the tracks every morning, on time,' says former coach Nabajit Malakar. She would travel 140 km daily to Guwahati to practise, sometimes returning as late as 11 p.m.

Her father, once a fast runner himself, bought her the first pair of spiked running shoes she owned. They cost ₹1,200, a huge sum for the family. He also encouraged her to participate in the Asian Games, even though it meant skipping her Higher Secondary exams.

At the IAAF race, Hima ran at an even pace before a sudden burst of speed in the last 100 m stretch. She doesn't care about medals and world rankings, but about timing. 'I am running after time. Once I get that, gold medals will run after me,' she says.

Before a race, Hima often utters the phrase, *phali dim*. It loosely translates to 'I will conquer' – and conquer she has. After IAAF, she won a gold and two silver medals at the 2018 Asian Games in Jakarta, clocking 50.79 seconds in the 400 m final, her personal best.

What does *phali dim* mean?

These women are beacons of hope for girls who dream of winning **laurels** for India. Their stories of **triumph** raise the hope that the day is not far when Indian women, in greater numbers, will bring India sporting glory.

intervention: action taken to improve or help a situation
spikes: shoes with sharp extensions on the outer sole for better grip
laurels: honourable distinctions
triumph: victory

Comprehension

A. Answer the questions.

1. Which event made Mary Kom the most successful boxer in the history of the Women's World Boxing Championships?
2. What are the qualities that make up for Mary Kom's lack of height?
3. Why did Mary keep her interest in boxing a secret from her father? How did he find out?
4. Which gymnastic move did Dipa perform and why?
5. What setback did Dipa face after the Olympics and how did she make her comeback?
6. What is 'second nature' for Hima Das? Which childhood incident illustrates it?
7. What role did Hima's father play in her progress in sports?

B. Answer the questions with reference to context.

1. *Her dreams came true in 2012 when she clinched a bronze at the London Olympics. She received a standing ovation as she left the hall.*
   a. Whose dreams came true?
   b. Which accolade had she achieved in 2008, prior to the London Olympics? Why was this victory special?
   c. Why do you think she received a 'standing ovation' as she left the hall?
2. *Adversity was a constant companion.*
   a. Whose constant companion was adversity?
   b. What were the problems faced by the person? How did she overcome them?
   c. What happened to her in 2007?
3. *His intervention got Hima, who had been playing football in local tournaments, into athletics.*
   a. Whose intervention got Hima into athletics? What had she been doing earlier?
   b. Where did 'he' notice Hima and what action did he take?
   c. After getting into athletics, what were the obstacles that Hima faced in 2017?

Life Skills and Values — determination, perseverance

1. There is a common element in the stories of the three sportswomen. What do you think it is, and why is it praiseworthy?
2. Dipa Karmakar took a risk in choosing the Produnova. Do you think it was wise to take a risk which could have ended her career? Would you take such a risk if you were in her place? Give reasons for your answer.

Vocabulary

collocations

A **collocation** is a group of two or more words that are often used together.

Examples: second nature   serious injury

A. Match the words in Column A with those in Column B to form collocations. Then make sentences of your own with them.

Column A	Column B
1. cast	a. cold
2. make	b. a secret
3. pay	c. exercise
4. bitterly	d. a wish
5. keep	e. time
6. save	f. a spell
7. regular	g. attention

B. Choose the correct one word substitutes for the given phrases.

anonymous	carnivores	matinee	autobiography
irreparable	centenarian	champion	optimist

1. A person who is always hopeful and positive: __________
2. Something from or by a person or author, whose name is unknown: __________
3. A damage that cannot be undone: __________
4. Creatures who eat only meat: __________
5. A person who is over a hundred years old: __________
6. A film show that is held in the afternoon: __________
7. A person who performs the best at a particular skill or sport: __________
8. An account of a person's life, written by that person: __________

Grammar

active and passive voice

Read these sentences.

In 2007, Dipa won the Junior National Championships for the first time.
In 2007, the Junior National Championships was won by Dipa for the first time.

In the first sentence, the subject *Dipa* is performing the action, *won*. It is in the active voice.
In the second sentence, the subject *Junior National Championships* is receiving the action, *was won*. The object in the first sentence is the subject in the second. The sentence is in the passive voice.

In a sentence, when the doer of the action is the subject, it is said to be in the **active voice**. When the subject of a sentence is the person or thing which receives the action, the sentence is said to be in the **passive voice**.

When a sentence is rewritten in the passive voice, we add *by* before the doer of the action. If the doer of the action is understood or unknown, it is not mentioned.

Example: We lost the match. (active voice)
The match was lost. (passive voice)

Remember that in the passive voice, we use *be* and the past participle form of the verb. Sometimes, the personal pronoun also changes its form in the passive.

Example: The lady took *him* to the market. (active voice)
He was taken to the market by the lady. (passive voice)

A. Identify whether these sentences are in the active or passive voice. Then change the sentences in the active voice to the passive voice and vice versa.

1. My mother baked a chocolate cake for my birthday.
2. The gardener takes care of the flower beds.
3. We were taught English by Mrs Saunders.
4. The match has been suspended because of sudden rain.
5. The thief was caught by the police.
6. The museum in-charge answered all our questions patiently.
7. Do you know the answer to this question?
8. Her dance performance was appreciated.

question tags

A **question tag** is a short question that confirms the information or opinion expressed in the main statement. They are often used in informal, spoken English.

Examples: Mary Kom is a boxer, **isn't she**?
Dipa did not win an Olympic medal, **did she**?

Remember that if the main sentence is affirmative, then the question tag is negative. If the main sentence is negative, then the question tag is positive.

B. Fill in the blanks with suitable question tags.

1. Your birthday is in March, ______________?
2. We are going to Bhutan this year, ______________?
3. Meher is a lovely dancer, ______________?
4. The athlete couldn't pull off that jump, ______________?
5. Let us hire a new trainer for the dog, ______________?
6. The sisters love their pets, ______________?
7. They did not inform us about the change in timing, ______________?
8. Mira does not have school tomorrow, ______________?

Study Skills

Spelling

words with *au* sound

Read these words aloud.

born flaw called vault

The highlighted letters in these four words produce the same *au* sound.

Read the clues and write the words with 'au' sound.

1. something in its uncooked, natural state ______________
2. a small electric lamp: ______________
3. to say something: ______________
4. a white powder used to season food: ______________
5. the hooked nail in a bird or an animal's feet: ______________
6. the opposite of *tall*: ______________
7. a place where clothes are washed: ______________
8. a place said to be inhabited by ghosts: ______________

Listening

listening for information

Listen to a passage about the Indian women's basketball team and answer the questions.

1. At which tournament did India win its fourth straight title?
2. Who did they play against? What was the final score?
3. Where did the match take place?
4. What was the name of the substitute player?
5. Who took advantage of early chances for India?
6. Who was the Croatian player who tested the Indian defence?

Speaking

giving a speech

You will be giving the opening speech on your school's Annual Sports Day. The topic is the importance of women's participation in sports. Prepare and deliver your speech. You may include these points in your speech.

- Women can excel in sports, just as they have in other fields.
- There is a pressing need for better facilities for women in sports.
- Globally more and more women are excelling in different sporting arenas.
- Sports should be available as a career option for women, just as it is for men.

Writing

Write a newspaper report about a recent win by India at the World Badminton Championships.

Keep the following points in mind while writing the report.

- The title/headline of your report should be short and catchy.
- It should start with the date and place.
- It should be to-the-point; avoid expressing personal opinions.

Useful words and phrases

- The atmosphere was electric…
- The crowd was eagerly waiting…
- The players walked out…
- The first set…
- The second set…
- There was nail-biting tension…
- The winner dropped to his/her knees…

Now I can... — Self-Assessment

- o read and appreciate stories of determination and courage of sportswomen.
- o use collocations and one word substitutes.
- o understand and use the active and passive voice, and question tags in sentences.
- o spell words with the *au* sound correctly.
- o give a speech, and write a newspaper report.

Read at Leisure

Throw Like a Girl: This book by Jennie Finch and Ann Killion talks about how today's girls should live, touching topics related to fitness and ways of integrating the lessons of sport into life.

Letters to a Young Gymnast: This autobiographical book by Nadia Comaneci describes how she harnessed her inner strength and determination to become one of the greatest gymnasts of her time.

didactic poem

18 A Psalm of Life

Henry Wadsworth Longfellow

Reading

What do you think your role in this world is? Do you feel that it is important to do something notable which will make people remember us in future? Read this poem which tells us how we can live a meaningful life.

Tell me not, in **mournful** numbers,
Life is but an empty dream!—
For the soul is dead that **slumbers**,
And things are not what they seem.

Life is real! Life is **earnest**!
And the grave is not its goal;
Dust thou art, to dust returnest,
Was not spoken of the soul.

In the world's broad field of battle,
In the **bivouac**[1] of life,
Be not like dumb, driven cattle!
Be a hero in the **strife**!

Lives of great men all remind us
We can make our lives **sublime**,
And, departing, leave behind us
Footprints on the sands of time[2];

Footprints, that perhaps another,
Sailing o'er life's **solemn main**,
A **forlorn** and shipwrecked brother,
Seeing, shall **take heart** again.

Let us, then, be up and doing,
With a heart for any fate;
Still achieving, still pursuing,
Learn to **labour** and to wait.

Food for thought

Dust thou art, to dust returnest is a well-known phrase from the *Book of Common Prayer*. It means that the human body is created from the earth, and after death, the physical body becomes one with the earth again.

Literary terms

1. This is an example of **alliteration**, as the 'b' sound is repeated in words placed close to each other.
2. This is a **metaphor**, where a person's achievements and the effect they leave behind are compared to footprints on a sandy beach.

mournful: sad
slumbers: sleeps
earnest: serious
bivouac: a place used for military encampment
strife: struggle
sublime: of very high quality, causing great admiration
solemn: serious
main: (here) broad sea of life
forlorn: sad and lonely
take heart: find fresh courage
labour: work hard

About the poet

Henry Wadsworth Longfellow (1807–1882) was a scholar, poet and novelist of the nineteenth century, famous for works like *The Song of Hiawatha*, *Voices of the Night* and *Evangeline*. He wrote lyric poems which were loved for their musical quality.

Understanding the poem

A. Complete the sentences with words and phrases from the poem.

1. The poet does not want to be told that life is ____________________.
2. He says that the world is like a ____________________.
3. He encourages the reader to be a ____________________.
4. He says that lives of great men remind us that ____________________.
5. In the end, he says that we should learn to ____________________.

B. Answer the questions with reference to context.

1. *Life is real! Life is earnest!/And the grave is not its goal...*
   a. What does the poet mean when he describes life as real and earnest?
   b. What does 'grave' symbolize here?
   c. What message about life and soul is the poet trying to convey to the readers?
2. *We can make our lives sublime,*
   And, departing, leave behind us
   Footprints on the sands of time;
   a. How can we make our lives 'sublime'?
   b. What does the line 'footprints on the sands of time' mean? Name the literary device used.
   c. Why is it important that we leave something behind in life?
3. *...A forlorn and shipwrecked brother,/Seeing, shall take heart again.*
   a. Who is the 'brother' being referred to here?
   b. Why do you think the poet has used words like 'forlorn' and 'shipwrecked'?
   c. Identify the figure of speech used here. How shall the brother 'take heart' again?

Life Skills and Values — positivity and optimism

1. What problems do you think a person has to face while trying to live life to the fullest?
2. Explain the meaning of the stanza 'In the world's broad field of battle... Be a hero in the strife!'

Vocabulary

metaphor

A **metaphor** is a figure of speech in which a person or thing is compared to another, otherwise unrelated person or thing.

In a metaphor, the comparison is usually implied, and not directly stated using the words *as* or *like*, as is done in the case of a simile.

Example: Life is but an empty dream (Life is being compared to a dream that has no meaning.)

A. Read the passage carefully. Then, underline the metaphors and circle the similes.

Breakfast on Sundays is like a movie production in my house. The sky is a blue umbrella by the time the breakfast table is laid. The sunbeams fall across the table like the stripes on a tiger's back. The aroma of good food wafts around the house like a happy ghost inviting everyone to join in. Buttered pancakes are piled on a plate like a golden mountain. Mother, a goddess in the kitchen, bustles around the table, handing out heaped plates of food to everybody.

archaic words

Read these lines.
Dust **thou art**, to dust **returnest** (thou - you; art - are; returnest - return)
Sailing **o'er** life's solemn main (o'er - over)

The highlighted words are no longer in everyday use or have lost a particular meaning in current usage. They are **archaic words**.

B. Match these archaic words with their meanings. You may use your dictionary.

Words	Meanings
1. hearken	a. you
2. hither	b. I think
3. begone	c. listen
4. thither	d. may be
5. thee	e. there
6. methinks	f. before
7. ere	g. here
8. mayhap	h. go away

Activity

writing a poem

Look at the picture and write a short poem on it, on the theme 'dreams and hopes for the future'.

Useful words and phrases	
rise	succeed
grow	aim
dream	effort
future	belief

Now I can... — Self-Assessment

- read and understand a poem about leading life in a positive manner.
- identify metaphors and match archaic words with their meanings.
- write a short poem.

Read at Leisure

The Character of the Happy Warrior: This poem by William Wordsworth is about an inspirational leader who is able to retain the innocent enthusiasm and enjoyment of life, despite his responsibilities.

Equipment: This poem by Edgar Guest is addressed to a young boy, telling him to search within himself for his own strengths and abilities.

Project 3

A. In the chapter *The Theft of the Ruby*, you read about some food traditions related to Christmas. These customs may vary from country to country. Work in pairs and find out about food traditions related to festivals in any three countries of your choice. Make a collage with images and present it to the rest of the class. Remember to include the story behind each tradition too.

Interesting food traditions

- Oysters for Christmas in France
- Latkes for Hanukkah
- Dried or salted fish in Norway
- Bumbong (sweet rice pudding) in the Philippines

B. You read about Indian sportswomen who are doing our country proud in the chapter *India's Shining Girls*. Find out about the following sportswomen who have been Indian icons and complete the table.

Sportswomen	Sport awards	Notable achievements
1. Mithali Raj		
2. Sania Mirza		
3. Saina Nehwal		
4. P. T. Usha		
5. Shiny Abraham		
6. Bula Chowdhury		

Literary Genres and Terms

Literary Genres

The stories and poems which you have read in this book are of various types. The following are some common kinds.

Prose

A **fable** is a story with a moral lesson at the end. In fables, animals, plants and non-living things often speak like humans.

A **fairy tale** is a story which has magical events and creatures like fairies, elves and goblins.

A **short story** narrates a tale that is only a few pages long.

A **folktale** is a story common among people who come from the same background. It is usually passed on in the form of an oral tale.

Humour is a type of literature which makes people laugh. A humorous story often has fun and excitement as its main elements.

Mythology includes traditional stories about gods that were told by people to explain natural events like lightning, and night and day.

Non-fiction is a type of literature that is based on real events rather than imaginary ones.

A **graphic story** is a story that is presented in comic-strip format.

An **adventure** is a type of story or book which has a lot of action, danger, risk and excitement.

Mystery is a genre of fiction that deals with the solution of a crime or the uncovering of secrets.

A **biography** is the story of a person's life, written by someone else.

A **fantasy** is a story or a novel which has a strange or other-worldly setting or characters. It often involves magic and supernatural creatures.

A **parable** is a short story that teaches a moral lesson. Unlike fables, the characters in a parable are human beings.

Poetry

A **nonsense poem** is a light-hearted, rhyming poem with characters in unusual situations. In such poems, everyday things are often described in an unusual way.

A **lyric poem** is a short poem whose main purpose is to express emotions or a state of mind. It does not depict actions or events.

Light verse is humorous poetry, usually dealing with playful themes and aimed at amusing the reader. It often uses literary devices, especially puns and alliterations.

A **narrative poem** is a type of verse which tells a story. It often has the voices of the characters in the story, along with the narrator's voice.

A **didactic poem** is a poem which teaches a moral lesson.

Literary Terms

Literary terms include common figures of speech. These are the various techniques writers use to convey their message.

A **simile** is a figure of speech in which someone or something is compared to a very different person or thing using *as* or *like*. **Example:** He is as strong as an ox.

Alliteration is the use of the same letter or sound at the beginning of words in a sentence, especially in poetry. **Example:** Three grey geese were grazing in a green field.

Onomatopoeia is the use of words whose pronunciation is similar to the sounds they represent. **Examples:** thump, whoosh, swish

Personification is a way of imagining non-living things or abstract ideas as human beings with thoughts, actions and emotions. **Example:** The glass danced up and down on the table.

A **metaphor** is a figure of speech in which a person or thing is compared to another, otherwise unrelated person or thing by stating that they are the same in a particular way. **Example:** Pamela is the apple of her father's eye.

Imagery is the use of descriptive language to create pictures or images in the minds of readers. It appeals to the five senses. **Example:** It was a dark and stormy night.

Repetition is the use of the same word or phrase at intervals to give stress on a particular idea. **Example:** Listen to the words of wisdom,/Listen to the words of warning

Refrain is the repeated use of a line in different stanzas of a poem to create rhyme. **Example:** What does he plant who plants a tree?/He plants a friend of sun and sky... What does he plant who plants a tree?/He plants cool shade and tender rain

A **pun** is a literary device which plays on the different meanings of the same word, or the similar sound of different words, to produce a humorous effect. **Example:** I've often watched my pillow fight.

Irony is a figure of speech in which the real meaning is exactly the opposite of what is said. **Example:** Have anything you wish! (said after banning every type of food item).